Die with Memories, Not Dreams

TOM PARKER

For you Mum, you've always
encouraged me to chase my dreams

CONTENTS

INTRODUCTION

Lesson #1: Save yourself

"No one saves us but ourselves. No one can, and no one may. We ourselves must walk the path" Buddha

When a painful change enters your life without warning, it throws your entire world into chaos. You're going through life thinking you've got it all figured out, but then something happens that knocks you off course. All of a sudden, you're heading in a direction that you don't want to be going. You reach a critical point in your life where you can continue down this path of suffering and misery and still not change the events of the past, or choose to accept what has happened, stop the pain and make the decision to save yourself.

When contemplating this myself, I had a sudden realisation. If I continued down the path of suffering, I would be guaranteed a miserable life. But if I decided to change something, I would at least have a chance of making a better life for myself. It was a hugely liberating feeling because I had nothing to lose and everything to gain. I decided to make a change. I had no idea how, so I wrote a list of 100 things I wanted to do in a year. My thinking was that if I could achieve half of what was on my list, I'd be in a much different place by the end of the year. And I was right; I had the best year of my life. I completed my first triathlon, went scuba diving for the first time, started a business, and read over 50 self-development books to name a few things. I went to some fantastic places, and I made some great memories but more than all of that I learnt a lot of valuable life lessons along the way. This book includes all those lessons that have helped me turn my life around.

When I started working on my list, it was never my intention to write this book. Still, as I discovered powerful new ways to transform my life for the better, I began to form an operating manual for how to live my life, something I could refer to when I needed inspiration or guidance. This operating manual consisted of pages and pages of disorganised notes, so I decided to write 100 lessons based on my experiences and what I'd learnt. Self-help author Zig Ziglar talks about writing a book to get your thoughts clear about life, and this was what I was doing. He writes:

"I think everybody ought to write a book. I don't necessarily believe you ought to get the book published or make any effort to get the book published but you ought to write a book. I'll tell you

what the title of it should be: What I think you ought to do to get the most out of life. Let me make a strong statement. If my book See You At The Top which has now sold over 2 million copies, if this book had never sold a single copy I would still say this is the most profitable thing that I have ever done if it had never sold a single copy. As I was writing this book, I realised what I was doing was clarifying my thinking about what life was all about. For the first time, I really discovered what I felt was important, and the research uncovered a number of things that I'd never been able to articulate".

The process of getting my thoughts onto paper and organising and presenting them in a way that can benefit others has helped me clarify and articulate what I consider to be important in life. It has taken me to a new level of my life where everything seems much clearer and has made me a much calmer and happier person. I can view life through a different lens and don't worry or stress about meaningless stuff. I now hold in my hands the knowledge that has taken me from the worst point to the happiest and most fulfilled point in my life.

We are all in pursuit of something. Some call it success, others happiness or fulfilment. Whatever you are looking for from life is unique to you, and your actions are ultimately an attempt to find this feeling and make it last. It is the feeling where we experience the best from life (throughout this book, I will be talking about this concept and will use the term success to define it). You can imagine your journey through life as being like the diagram below. We start at point A and are working to experience the best from life at point E. But along the way, events happen (point B) that knock us off course and away from our destination.

When this happens, you must be strong enough to change something, or your life can very quickly continue down the path of pain and suffering. This first lesson is about point C on the diagram – change starts with you. If you want to save yourself, you must create your path and be the person who makes that change happen.

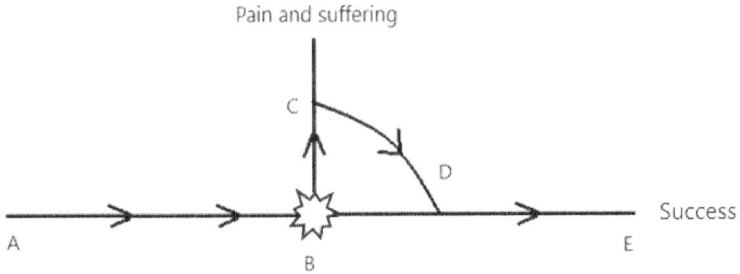

Pain and suffering

C

D

A

B

E

Success

There are two types of people: those who make their path and those who simply drift along and let their lives happen to them. Those who drift along will follow wherever the river of life takes them, believing that life is something that happens to them and their results are due to external forces outside their control. As a result of this perceived lack of control, they believe that they have no choice and feel helpless. So, when something happens to them, they get hit off course and keep going down the wrong path. Do you know where most of these people end up? On the rocks. They go with the flow and then end up complaining about where they floated. If you're reading this thinking that you're a drifter, it doesn't have to be that way. You can create your path in life. It starts with a choice. If you want a change, you have to be the person who makes that change happen. No one else will save you. You must be the person to walk the path. The first step (and first lesson) in this book is that you can save yourself. Pick up a paddle and start steering towards the life you want.

<u>What are the lessons in this book about?</u>

Whatever success means to you, the core theme of this book is helping you get there. I will share the lessons that have helped me go from Point B to C to D to E and hope that you can relate in some way to benefit yourself. This book offers a mix of philosophy, science, mindset hacks, and practical tools for daily use that I consider to be essential to reaching success. Each lesson starts with a quote followed by my attempt to tell a story, provide context, ask a question, or put forward an exercise so you may find a deeper understanding of whatever it is you are looking for. The lessons are designed so that they are easy to work through with one or two key take-home messages which are summarised at the end of each lesson. Complete the exercises and think about how you can put what you learn into action in the areas of your life you'd like to change. I have developed a set of supplementary documents you can print out and use as templates for the different exercises. I haven't reinvented anything; I've simply used the information available from some of history's greatest minds. I will put forward a philosophy designed to help you answer three fundamental questions:

1. Who am I?
2. What do I want?
3. How can I get it?

The book is, therefore, divided into three main sections looking first at yourself, then your desires, and finally, how to bring them into reality. Within each section, there are central themes:

1. Who am I?
   a. Understand where your behaviours originate from
   b. Understand what you can do to change your behaviours
   c. Look at how we perceive the world around us and how, by controlling our perceptions, we can gain mental clarity
   d. Understand what is within our control and develop the perspective to deal with anything the world puts before you and let go of what you can't control.
   e. You will see the only things you can truly control are your thoughts, attitude, and actions
   f. The importance of discipline and habit in shaping your actions
2. What do I want?
   a. What is most important to you
   b. Why those things matter most to you
   c. Your purpose
   d. Your goals
3. How can I get it?
   a. Focus on the decisions and actions we take and to what end. Better directed efforts are more effective actions.
   b. Overcoming fear, perfectionism, and procrastination

    c. How to organise your work and when to do it
    d. How to monitor your progress
    e. Defining and celebrating success
    f. Feeding back the lessons you learn

I hope that by the end of the book, you have learnt how to take complete control over your path in life and how to become a stronger, happier, and more confident person in every area of your life that is important to you. The lessons have helped me turn my life around, and I know it can do the same for you.

Lesson summary:

1. Events will alter your trajectory through life, and some will guide you down dark paths.
2. Don't drift along, be strong enough to save yourself by being the person to make change happen.

Lesson #2: Find your way back

"Sometimes when you lose your way, you find yourself" Mandy Hale

Once you've made the decision that you want to change your life in some way, the next challenge is getting back on course, which is represented by point D on the diagram. Deciding to change is one thing but making that change happen is something else. Most of us want to change but don't know how to do it. In many of the lessons in this book, I will share how I did it, and hopefully, you can learn something which you can apply to your situation. But for now, this lesson focuses on the very first step.

If you feel lost in life and don't know which direction to turn, you're not alone. If you feel trapped in your situation and don't know how to get out, it's like being in a dark forest and not knowing which direction to head. Feeling lost and not knowing where you are or what direction to head in is scary. But if you get lost in a forest and can't see the path, does standing still help you find your way out? No, you must start walking. It doesn't matter which direction you walk. Whichever way you go, you'll eventually find a way out of the woods.

Take one step at a time, and as you start making progress, you will see things that you'll either want to move closer to or further away from. You have a compass inside of you, but most just don't know how to read it. The compass will always point you towards things that you're interested in, curious about, or energised by. We will explore these things in the book to direct you to where you want to be. Once you start walking, you're going to learn what you need to take the next step and the step after that until you reach your destination. The truth is you're never truly lost if you're moving; you're lost only for as long as you're standing still, spinning in place. You will find your way back. I did. So will you. However lost and hopeless you feel right now, we will walk this path together, and you will find your way back. So, stop spinning, and let's start walking.

Lesson summary:

1. You're only lost when you're spinning on the spot.
2. As soon as you start moving, you're no longer lost.

PART 1 - WHO AM I?

"The only person you are destined to become is the person you decide to be" Ralph Waldo Emerson

Lesson #3: The place to start is with yourself. If you're right, your world will be right.

"Knowing yourself is the beginning of all wisdom" Aristotle

I came across the following fable and it seemed like the perfect place to start the book. One day, a vicar was preparing his service. He was home alone with his son, who was bored with nothing to do. The vicar picked up a magazine and flicked through it until he came to a page showing a map of the world. He took the page from the magazine, ripped it into lots of pieces and threw them on the floor. He then challenged his son to put the pieces back together for a reward. The vicar hoped this would keep his son occupied for most of the morning but within an hour

9

the boy was boasting that he had completed the puzzle and wanted his prize. The vicar was amazed that the son completed it so soon and asked how he did it. The son replied "It was easy. On the other side of the page, there was a picture of a man. I just put the man back together, then turned it over. I thought that if I got the man right, the world would be right". The vicar smiled and replied "Well done son, you've given me an idea for my service. If a man is right, his world will be right".

After hearing this story, I knew the first section of this book had to be getting yourself 'right' before thinking about what you want or how to get it. Because if you're right, the rest will fall into place. Most who seek success focus on the what and the how. But start with the who and ask, who do I need to become to achieve success? Success is something you attract by the person you become. To have more, you first must become more.

Lesson summary:

1.   Get yourself right, and your world will be right.

Understanding who you are means understanding your personality. Psychologists use the word personality to describe consistencies in a person's behaviour across various situations. Therefore, understanding yourself comes down to understanding what influences your behaviour. Our subconscious mind controls many of the behaviours that lead to our actions, and we unknowingly accept this as the way things are. But by developing self-awareness, you can understand why you do the things you do and take action to change your behaviour, so you act in a way that best serves you.

Whether nature or nurture influences your behaviour is debatable. But the either-or solution seems far too simplistic to describe you. You are not the result of one or the other, but both. Throughout this section, we will try to understand your behaviours within the context of the following two themes:

1. Evolution/genetics (nature)

2. Environment/conditioning (nurture).

I will introduce both themes in the next two lessons.

Lesson #4: We are living in the modern world with a stone-age brain

"Unless we base our sense of identity upon the truth of who we are, it is impossible to attain true happiness" Brenda Shoshanna

This lesson briefly explains how evolution has led to your behaviours. It is critical to many of the lessons throughout this book, as it explains why you act in ways that are not in your best interest. When I talk about evolution here, I mean our recent evolution. It goes back approximately six million years to when we evolved from our apelike ancestors. It is during this time that many of our behaviours (what we would call human nature) evolved.

Our apelike ancestors faced daily threats and challenges to their survival and reproduction. Through natural genetic variation, some individuals had characteristics that provided them with an advantage. For example, a taller, stronger individual will be able to fight off threats more easily than a shorter, weaker person. As such, the advantaged individual had a higher chance of survival and was more likely to be successful in producing offspring and transferring their genes. Over millions of years, any physical characteristics which provided an advantage were passed down the generations.

It's not only our physical traits that have evolved but also our behaviour or human nature. For example, fear as a behavioural trait offered an evolutionary advantage because those individuals who experienced it had a higher chance of surviving and reproducing. As such, that trait has been passed down the generations and now forms part of human nature.

But these features of human nature evolved because they were adaptive in the environment in which our prehistoric ancestors lived. They made complete sense in that environment as they offered a survival advantage. But they may not make sense in the modern world.

Anything resembling modern civilisation is thought to have formed around 10,000 years ago. This timeframe is the blink of an eye in evolutionary terms, and biologists mostly agree that our brains have not changed in that timeframe. As a result, we have the same brain that our prehistoric ancestors had but in a much different environment. We are living in the modern world with a stone-age brain. This fact helps explain many of the human behaviours that are part of our nature which are not beneficial to us today. I will come back to this explanation as the basis for many of our negative behaviours.

But don't think that because these behaviours are part of human nature that they have to rule our lives. We have a choice; we can control our behaviours and don't have to act as human nature designed us. It's more difficult if it involves an evolutionary designed system, and it just means that we must try harder, not that we shouldn't try at all. First, we must become aware of why our human nature leads us to behave in ways that aren't always in our best interests. From there, we can look to behave differently, in ways that will serve us best.

Lesson summary:

1. The requirements of a completely different environment from the modern world designed your brain.
2. This fact explains many of our behaviours which are not beneficial to us however we can consciously choose to behave otherwise.

Lesson #5: You are capable of reconditioning yourself

"Old ways won't open new doors" Unknown

To train fleas, you put them in a jar and screw on the lid. The fleas will jump up to escape but will hit the top, over and over again. They continue to jump for a while, hitting the lid of the jar then suddenly, they don't jump as high. You can then take the top off and the fleas, who are perfectly capable of jumping out of the jar, stay trapped in there. They don't jump out because they've conditioned themselves to jump lower than the height of the jar and now that's all they can do.

We behave in the same way. We start in life with no conditioning, but along the way, life happens to us. We bump our head a few times just as the fleas do and eventually don't jump to those same heights. Life conditions us to jump a little lower. The trouble with this is we get trapped in the jar and cannot get out. Despite there being no limit on what we can achieve, suddenly we place restrictions on ourselves. Most of us want to change; we just can't reverse a life's worth of conditioning. We know what we should do yet somehow can't do it.

The other part of what makes you who you are is the environment in which you were raised and live. It is the nurture part, and it has conditioned you to behave a certain way. We all vary from one another in the environment that we grew up in. No two people share the same experiences in life. If evolution and genetics determine the material we are made from, then our experiences determine the shape into which we mould. While we can't change what we're made from, we can change how we're moulded. In the same way that exercise can condition your body to change shape, we are also capable of reconditioning our minds. It just requires the right knowledge and some persistence.

We are complex creatures and all very different. Therefore, it is not possible to write everything everybody needs to know in one book. Answering the question "why did you turn out the way you have?" is not straightforward. But I will put forward some information that hopefully makes sense in explaining this. Our evolution and our environment lead to the behaviours that hold us back. We are disadvantaged by our starting point (human nature), and life experiences further disadvantage many of us. In the first section of the book, we will work to understand the life experiences that have conditioned us to behave the way we do. Luckily, the answer to the question "what can I do to change?" is easier to answer. Just as you've been conditioned by your experiences, with the right knowledge and mindset, you can reverse your conditioning and adopt new behaviours that will serve you. By the end, I hope you've learnt what you need to escape the jar you're trapped in.

This section is divided into three chapters:

1. Thoughts and beliefs
2. Attitude
3. Actions

Your thoughts and beliefs form your attitudes, and your attitudes lead to your actions. If your internal layers determine your actions, then greater clarity of these aspects will lead to more effective actions. We discuss each layer in-depth and explore practical techniques to help you gain absolute clarity on who you are. After reading this section of the book, you will be able to answer the following questions:

1. Why do I think the things I do?
2. What can I do to change my thoughts?
3. What beliefs do I have and where do they originate?
4. How can self-limiting beliefs be changed?
5. What is within my control?
6. Do my attitudes best serve my goals?

7. How can I develop my discipline and habits, so my actions serve my goals?

Lesson summary:

1. Life has conditioned you to behave in a certain way, which might not be in your best interest.
2. We are capable of reconditioning ourselves.

1 THOUGHTS & BELIEFS

"The world as we have created is a process of our thinking, to change the world we must change our thinking" Albert Einstein

More than anyone, we talk to ourselves the most. There is near-constant chatter inside your head. But have you considered who's doing the talking, where thoughts originate, or who controls them? It is crucial to answer these questions because your thoughts lead to your beliefs, and your beliefs subsequently lead to your actions. And it is your actions which ultimately determine the life you lead. Therefore, understand and know how to control your thoughts, and you control your life.

Lesson #6: Thoughts and beliefs are the traffic lights of your life

"Whether you think you can, or you think you can't, you're right" Henry Ford

Imagine your path through life is like a car journey. As you drive along, your route is blocked at specific points by red lights, forcing you to travel a different way. In some places, you get stuck unable to progress any closer to your destination. These traffic lights are like your thoughts and beliefs; when they are green, you can move on and go to new places. But when they are red, you are forced to take another route or worse, get stuck entirely.

Throughout life, it can seem like you come up against the same barriers time after time. You might think you aren't good enough or don't deserve success, so feel stuck, unable to move forward. But you're not stuck. You're just committed to specific patterns of behaviour because you think they've helped you in the past. But those behaviours have become more harmful than helpful. The reason you aren't moving forward is you keep applying an old formula to a new level in your life. You can't change the fruit without first changing the root, so don't expect your life to change without changing your thoughts and beliefs. Therefore, the first stage on the path to success is to examine your thoughts and beliefs so you can be sure that they lead to attitudes and actions that will guide you to success. By the end of this chapter, you will know how to change your traffic lights from red to green. We will examine your old patterns and provide specific, actionable steps to help you change them from limiting to empowering.

In this chapter, we will go back to the basics and answer questions such as:

1. What is thought, and why do we do it?
2. What behaviours do I act out as a result of human evolution and why?
3. What is the difference between my perceived reality and actual reality?
4. How did my beliefs form?
5. What false limiting beliefs do I have?
6. How can I overcome these and adopt new empowering beliefs?

Before we answer any of those questions, we will start by looking at your brain, how it evolved, and why it's not that well designed to deal with the modern world.

Lesson summary:

1. If you feel stuck in life, start by changing your thoughts and beliefs.

Lesson #7: Your brain is where it all starts and ends

"Many complain of their looks, but none of their brains" Proverb

Going back to the analogy in the previous lesson, we are all on a journey through life. But who's in control of the car? The driver is your brain. Everything you do in life originates as a thought in your brain. Every decision you make, every emotion you feel, and every belief you hold all start in your brain. But imagine that your driver had the fastest and most sophisticated car in the world, but all they did was listen to the radio. Or they took it off the road where it wasn't designed to go and wrecked it. Or they never learnt how to drive, so ended up hurting you and everyone around you. We commit all three of these mistakes with our brains. We don't use it to the best of its abilities, use it for the wrong reasons, and allow it to spin out of control with our thoughts, letting it ruin our lives and those of others. Would you expect to be a safe driver if you'd never taken any driving lessons? No, so it shouldn't be a massive surprise that we don't know how to use our brains in the correct way given we don't receive any training. Instead, we are guided and led by our nature. But there are several flaws to human nature, so allowing a faulty system to run our lives can lead to problems.

The primary function of your brain is to keep you safe and alive. And it does this very well. It can take in a vast amount of sensory information from your environment and scan that information to spot things that present a threat. It does this so well that you receive a lot of "false positive" threats where your brain will escalate a situation to threat level when it isn't necessary. Its ability to jump to the worst-case scenario was an obvious survival skill a few hundred thousand years ago when everyday threats were present. But features that were once an advantage for our survival, now act as the source of unnecessary suffering. It leads to some flaws in the modern world, including:

1. Your brain has a tendency for negativity
2. Your brain will try to tell you what to do
3. Your brain will not tell you the whole truth

Everything starts in the brain, but by becoming aware of these flaws and how they make us behave, we can put an end to our limiting behaviours. We will explore each of the design flaws mentioned above over the next three lessons. We will work to understand how your brain operates, why it works in the way it does, and how this leads to the flaws. Equipped with this knowledge, we can begin to change our traffic lights from red to green. So, let's explore each one of these flaws in detail and what they can mean for your experiences in life.

Lesson summary:

1. We receive no training on how to use our brains in the modern world and as such must rely on human nature to guide us.
2. As the brain evolved in a different environment with different requirements, it has some flaws when used in the modern world.

Lesson #8: Your brain has a tendency for negativity

"If you cannot be positive, then at least be quiet" Joel Osteen

The first flaw we will examine is your brain's tendency for negativity. As your brain's primary purpose is to keep you alive, it is always watching for what might pose a threat. Most of the information you receive is harmless, but in the unlikely event that it does pose a threat, your brain takes the approach that it's better to be safe than sorry. It's better to overact when no real danger is present than not to react at all when there is a threat. As a result, our default position is one of negativity.

Not only that, but due to the survival benefit that negative thoughts provide us, we tend to give them higher weight. So, you are generally more likely to make choices based on avoiding negative experiences rather than on attaining something positive. These aspects of human nature mean that most of the conversation in our head is negative. It can make it very difficult to achieve the things in life we want because our starting point is negativity. To overcome your negative default state and develop a positive mindset requires work. If you never learn how to develop a positive mindset, your default negative position may be your permanent position.

<u>Kill negative thoughts</u>

There are two levels to help you move away from your default negative state.

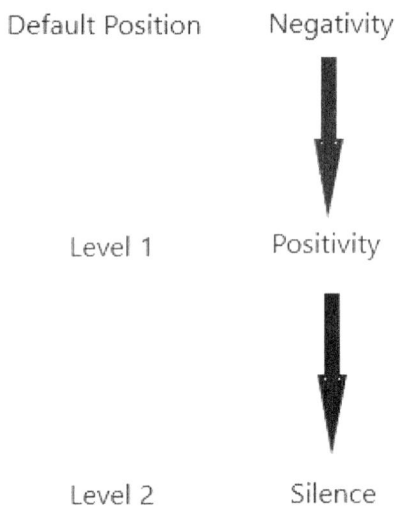

Default Position   Negativity

Level 1   Positivity

Level 2   Silence

The first is replacing the negativity with positivity. The second, more advanced level is replacing thoughts with silence. Given the quote at the start of the lesson, it may seem counterintuitive that level 1 is positivity, and silence is level 2 however, it is a difficult skill to silence your thoughts altogether. If you can reach this level, you can calmly observe the thoughts in your head, knowing the only power they have over you is the power you allow them.

1. Negative default state

i.   Observe your thoughts

The first stage in overcoming negativity is to acknowledge it. Track your thoughts for a day by marking each significant one as positive or negative on a piece of paper. This is one that leads to a feeling, action, or inaction that has consequences on your day. If you have a thought that makes you feel bad about yourself, mark it as a negative. If an idea leads you to take action on a goal, mark this as positive. Try this for a while and count the marks. Are most of them positive or negative? Most will have a negative majority. Research has shown that we tend to think approximately 60-70% negative thoughts. We have approximately 60,000 thoughts per day, so if 60-70% are negative, this equates to 36-43,000 per day. Have you thought about the effect that has on you? You are the product of your dominating thoughts, so think about the possible impact all those negative thoughts have on you. And the effect on your life if you started thinking more positively.

ii.   Observe the drama

Some of the negative thoughts will linger in your mind. These thoughts remain because of how they make you feel. So, when you notice yourself thinking the same negative thought over and over again, think about how it makes you feel. Observe the emotion that results from the thought and consider whether this is how you want to feel. Do nothing more than observe your negative thoughts and how they make you feel at this stage. When you have a greater awareness of these things, tell yourself that this is how you will continue to think and feel if you do nothing to change the situation.

2.   Level 1

If you decide you want better control over your thoughts, the first level of mind control is to change the voice in your head from negative to positive. Your brain is a serial processor, meaning that it can only focus on one thing at a time. So, when I say the words pink zebra, what do you think about? When you observe yourself thinking something negative, immediately replace that thought with something more positive. The act of thinking about the positive thing will replace the negative thought because your brain cannot focus on both elements. Use your library of positive experiences and feelings to pull positive thoughts.

If you can master this process, well done, you are in control. The next time you think about something negative that causes you suffering, you have an essential tool to focus on something more positive.

3. Level 2

You now know how to change the voice from negative to positive, but what if you want to take it to the next level and silence the voice altogether. A technique for doing this is to flood your brain with things it cannot think about, evaluate, or judge. Stuff it can only observe. Direct your attention to your immediate environment and see everything in your surroundings. Notice every tiny detail of everything around you. Then direct your focus on your body and pay close attention to how your body feels, your breathing, how your clothes feel on your skin. Take it all in. It is all the information that your brain has been filtering out so that it can focus on its thoughts. When you suddenly flood it with signals from the physical world, it doesn't get the chance to focus on its ideas. Instead, you're priming your brain to focus on what's right in front of you so that it has no room for thought. This is when you silence the voice, and it can feel uncomfortable as your brain isn't familiar with it. When you can master this technique, you can switch your thoughts on and off as you please. It is the ultimate form of mind control. We will expand on this technique in a later lesson on being present.

So much depends not upon on the world around you but on the thoughts you create about it. Learn to observe the dialogue and drama in your head calmly, and you gain clarity. You can watch your thoughts; knowing the only power they can gain over you is the power you grant them. You can tell your brain what to make of the world around it, not the other way around. You don't have to live in your negative default state.

Lesson summary:

1. Your brain's default is negativity, and we give greater weight to negative events and downplay positive events.
2. Work to move away from the negative default to positive thoughts and eventually silence.

Lesson #9: Your brain will try to tell you what to do

"The most courageous act is still to think for yourself" Coco Chanel

We think we are in control of the thoughts that pop into our mind, but maybe we aren't as in control as we think. We are certainly capable of being in control, but most of us aren't. Human nature controls many of us, and this can lead to unnecessary suffering and acting in ways that aren't in our best interest.

To see where you are right now, stop reading and take a few minutes to enjoy the peace. Did you manage to last a few minutes without something popping into your mind that you didn't want to think? Perhaps it was something you have to do today, or something coming up soon that you're not looking forward to. I'm guessing at some time during the last few minutes, something popped into your head that you didn't mean to think. Don't worry about it, this is what your brain does, and it's the second flaw which we will explore.

Your brain bombards you with a constant stream of thoughts that it decides could pose a threat to you. It is anxious about the uncertain future and views past experiences with negativity. As a result, the voice in your head will be saying things you don't need to be hearing. It will continuously criticise you, put you down, and compare you to others. It tells you not to do things that it perceives as risky in case you put yourself in danger. Day after day, we listen as it talks and talks. And the worst part is we think the voice talking is us. It's time to get clear on who's talking.

Who's actually talking?

It might seem like a strange question to ask. You might be thinking the voice you hear when a thought pops into your head is obviously you. But it's not. It's your stone-age brain presenting you with an idea that it considers important. Thought is a protection mechanism, trying to get you to act in a way that will ensure your survival. Less intelligent animals that are not capable of thinking ahead can only react when danger presents itself. But we can think ahead and can make plans to avoid danger altogether. It was essential for our survival thousands of years ago, but as we have already explored, your stone-age brain does not need to act in this way in the modern world.

So rather than receiving a thought from your brain and allowing it to control your behaviour, know that it doesn't have to be this way. Instead, think of it as your brain presenting information for you to consider. It is entirely up to you what you choose to do with that information.

Let's consider an example. Imagine you give a speech, and you mess up, and some people laugh at you. Your brain sees this as social rejection, and when our brains evolved, rejection from social groups was a significant threat. Your brain will present you with thoughts that you can't speak in public ever again as it threatens your life. If you hear these thoughts and believe that it is you speaking, you will probably listen to them and never speak in public again. But if you are aware of where these thoughts come from, you can consider and dismiss the information your brain is presenting to you. You know that, like anything, public speaking is a skill that you must practice, you will make mistakes, and if people laugh at you, it poses no threat to your survival whatsoever. So, the next time you hear a thought that limits you in some way, remember that this is just your stone-age brain presenting you with some information that it finds important. It is up to you what you do with that information.

<u>Where your brain functions very well</u>

There is a particular type of threat where your brain does function very well, and that is when there is an immediate danger. In this case, your brain will act without even consulting you. These are your reflexes. When you touch something hot, your arm will move away from the object before you're even aware of the threat. This is where our brains are protecting us from harm. So, it seems that the more something matters, the more thought is left out. Nature has excluded thought from these processes because it is unreliable.

So, what can we do? Firstly, accept that your brain will look after you and is in control when it comes to immediate danger. For less immediate danger, like your speech next month, remember that the function of your brain is to produce thoughts for you to consider. You always get to choose what to do with them. Your brain is an employee, working to provide you with information. You're the boss who takes that information and uses it for your best interests.

To function well in the modern world, you need to differentiate between the thoughts that are working for you and those that aren't. Your brain will present so much negativity and the threat of danger to you when really none exists. Whenever you step out of your comfort zone and strive for a better life, that voice will be there shouting "warning, we are in danger, you must go back where we are safe". And more often than not, we listen to this voice and hear it as fact. But when you realise where your thoughts come from, you can start to control how you respond to them. We can start saying more positive things that will drive us towards success.

Lesson summary:

1. Thought is a protection mechanism that originates from your brain to warn you of threats to your survival.
2. For critical survival skills, your brain does a good job; for everything else, it presents thoughts for your consideration. Remember that you're in control and get to choose what to do with those thoughts.

Lesson #10: Your brain will not tell you the whole truth

"People see what they want to see and what people want to see never has anything to do with the truth" Roberto Bolano

Through our senses, we take in information from the world, and it travels along our nervous system into the brain. The information it receives is so complex that the brain will use several tricks to help you interpret the world around you. It filters what information is taken in by only allowing the most critical information at that moment to be received. It fills in any gaps with assumptions that can often lead to us making up stories in our heads. And it will draw on your past experiences to predict the future.

The result of all these things is you don't see the world for what it is so you can often misinterpret things, and this can lead to suffering. This suffering is entirely unnecessary because we don't have to see the world in this way, where we distort events.

To reach success, you need to see beyond this and teach your brain to know the truth. When you do, you can overcome many of the thoughts and beliefs holding you back in life. The third and final flaw of your brain we will explore is how your brain interprets information from the world around you but does not tell you the whole truth. We will briefly touch on how it filters, assumes, and predicts, and how we can spot and overcome these flaws.

1. Filters

The world bombards you with sensory signals every second of the day. It comes in the form of light, sounds, smells, tastes, and touch signals. Every second, your body is taking in information from your environment and sending messages to the brain. Your brain does its best to make sense of all these signals; however, it cannot cope with everything at the same time. So, it does the same thing we would do if overloaded with work. It prioritises by filtering out details that are not relevant to the situation. Only by doing this can you focus on what is critical to the task at hand. For example, how often are you aware of the feel of your clothes on your skin? Probably not very often. Your brain filters out this information because it's not essential to what you're doing. You filter out so much. It is important to remember this because what you perceive is not the full picture. There is always more to the story than your brain is telling you.

2. Assumptions

Because your brain filters out so much, it creates gaps. So, it then goes on to fill these gaps with assumptions. How many times during your life have you made assumptions about things and they turned out to be wrong? Assumptions are pure guesswork and distort the truth. You can see this in action when you look at an optical illusion. What you visually perceive is interpreted by your brain as something which isn't real. This concept applies to all the senses, not only vision.

Many of the things in our world are so complex that they are beyond our capability to grasp fully. So, we simplify these things and fill in the blanks with assumptions. When we do this, we make up stories that edit a significant part of the truth. Due to our negative default, the stories we make up are more likely to be negative. But remember, if you hear yourself making assumptions and telling stories, these are not based on facts.

3. Predictions

A prediction is a specific form of assumption about a possible future event. Nothing is certain about the future, but your brain will still try to predict it. It will draw on previous experiences to build a story of possible outcomes. It takes things from your past that it sees as facts, then applies these to the future scenario you have in mind.

But here's the thing: when you give weight to your prediction and believe it to be accurate, you start acting as if that future has already happened. When we start acting in this way, more often than not, it results in making it happen. We begin to believe that our predictions are the truth and your brain now presents forecasts as a fact. But here's the fact: your predictions are nothing more than brain generated future possibilities. They have not happened. They are not the truth.

How to spot these flaws

To spot filtering, pay attention to your thoughts. Are you summarising a complex event in a short sentence? If so, ask what part of the story are you filtering out? Ask again and again until you see as much of the truth as you need for an objective view.

To spot assumptions, focus on what you can perceive through your senses. If you didn't sense it, then it's an assumption. Real events in your life start with the words "I saw", "I heard", "I felt" etc. Stories that we make up use words such as "I guess", "I assume", "I think".

Predictions are easy to spot because they are associated with the future tense. Therefore, the language you use will also be in the future tense. But remember, regardless of how convinced you are, if something hasn't happened yet, it's just a forecast, not the truth.

So far, we have focused on your brain and the role it plays in creating your thoughts. To summarise, your brain's primary objective is your survival. Because of this its default position is one of negativity. It generates thoughts to try to control you, but these are simply things for you to consider. You can choose how you respond to them. To top this all off, the information it receives from the outside world is often far from the truth because it filters, assumes, and predicts to make sense of the amount of information thrown at it. The remainder of the chapter will look at your beliefs. A belief is a conditioned perception that has taken hold in your subconscious mind due to the information and experiences you have been exposed to during your life. It is supported by sufficient evidence for you to say 'yes, I consider this to be true'. But, as with thoughts, you will see that not everything you believe to be true, actually is.

Lesson summary:

1. Your brain will filter reality and make assumptions and predictions.

2. Being aware of these flaws can help you gain greater clarity on life.

Lesson #11: Perception is not reality

"It's not necessarily reality that shapes us, but the lens through which your brain views the world that shapes your reality"
Shawn Achor

We each view the world through our unique lens. Over our lifetime, we take in information through this lens, and it shapes our idea of what reality is. We think that what we see through this lens is the one true reality. But it's not, it's merely our perception of the facts. Sadly, we allow our perceptions, rather than the facts, to shape us and form our beliefs.

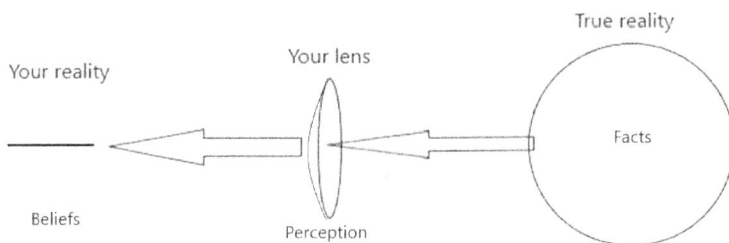

To help get your head around this, consider the fact that the world is round. We use our senses as tools to detect the world around us and see that the world is flat. Because we perceive the world as flat, we used to believe this to be true until it was proven otherwise. What we perceive, we believe is real. The lens through which you view the world distorts the facts of reality to create what you believe to be true. It means, your reality differs from actual reality, or in other words, your beliefs differ from the facts. But we see our reality as true reality and therefore see any limiting beliefs as facts. If we understand that our reality is different from true reality, you will see that many of the things you believe to be true about yourself are not. Over the rest of the chapter, we will see that our self-limiting beliefs are not facts.

Lesson summary:

1. Beliefs are perceptions of reality rather than true reality.

Lesson #12: The formation of your current belief system was out of your control

"Learning too soon our limitations, we never learn our powers" Mignon Mclaughlin

When you were born, you were a blank slate with no beliefs. As you move through life, you begin to interpret the world around you through your faulty lens. The interpretation of this information is far from perfect as we explored earlier in the chapter. It is the receiving and processing of information in the brain that leads to the formation of your beliefs. The part of the brain responsible for this is the subconscious mind.

The subconscious mind programmes our experiences, and over time you build up a database of references that form your beliefs. As we experience similar events, this repetition reinforces the references. Through repetitively thinking and acting out these things in life, your opinions solidify and turn into beliefs. When backed by emotion, the references that give rise to our beliefs become even stronger. Through repetition and emotion, eventually, we see the references as facts and believe them to be true.

You learn most of the beliefs about yourself as children, years before you develop the ability for critical thinking. Consider the example when parents tell their children that they can't do anything. As children, we cannot reject this statement, and so we accept it as truth. If parents repeatedly tell their children something, it reinforces the message. Negative emotions will almost certainly back it, and before long, the children believe this to be true. Therefore, a child's perceptions of themself are downloaded into the subconscious mind without the filters of the analytical conscious mind. So as kids, we download limiting and self-sabotaging beliefs which become our realities.

Consequently, we learn our fundamental perceptions about life and our role in it without us having the capacity to choose or reject them. As the subconscious mind is pre-programmed before we can decide what is stored, the database is one of misperception. Therefore, most of us live based on what we perceive as reality, rather than the truth. As limiting beliefs present us with a false view of reality that only exists in our head, we make choices that are not in our best interest. Deceiving ourselves with false truths and limiting beliefs could mean that we never reach our full potential.

Imagine your perfect life. Ask yourself why you aren't already living it, and I guarantee you will have one or more self-limiting beliefs. Through the inaccurate programming of the subconscious mind, you have developed beliefs that are preventing you from achieving success. You might consciously believe you can achieve success, but if your subconscious does not agree, you will struggle because it is much more powerful and will always win out. We tend to take our subconscious mind seriously and agree with it because we are wired to believe our thoughts regardless of whether they are helpful or accurate. Because of this, once a belief has formed, it can easily keep us trapped in the same negative cycle of behaviour. But beliefs can only keep us stuck for as long as we let them. If we continue to believe something to be true, it will continue to be our reality regardless of whether it is true. We can take control and start the process of re-conditioning our beliefs away from self-limiting and towards empowering. And that is what we will do over the remaining lessons of this chapter.

Common limiting beliefs

Below are ten examples of common limiting beliefs that could prevent you from reaching success. Using these examples, we will go through the process of reconditioning your subconscious mind. In the same way that you would condition your body with exercise, you can condition your mind with the techniques in this chapter.

1. "I'm not ready". We say this as if there is some kind of barometer to measure 'readiness' and we aren't yet at the level that we deem acceptable to ensure our safety.
2. "I don't know how". You don't know how to make progress and so do nothing.
3. "It's already been done". Thinking you have nothing unique to offer the world will result in no action.

4. "Who am I to try that?" Lack of self-confidence so you cannot see your unique talents or gifts.
5. "It's too late". Thinking you're too old. There are endless examples of people achieving massive success later in life.
6. "I'm not good enough". To not feel good enough is to feel a massive lack or void in life.
7. "I don't have time". We all have the same hours in a day.
8. "I can't be myself, or others will judge me". You'll probably be judged either way.
9. "I don't need or deserve to be successful". Everyone deserves success.
10. "I won't be accepted". Acceptance is another survival instinct. The chances that our prehistoric ancestors survived dramatically increased if they were part of a group. In the modern world, rejection does not pose a threat to your survival.

All of these limiting beliefs are the product of fear. You tell these things to yourself because when you've said them in the past, they have kept you safe. And your safety is the number one priority of your brain. But this safety comes at a cost: you take no action. Without action, you will remain in the same place. Fear is a subject we will look at in-depth later in the book. For now, we will focus on how to identify and let go of your limiting beliefs. Only by becoming aware of them can you change them and stop them from killing your dreams before you even begin.

Lesson summary:

1. Repetition and emotion convert references into beliefs in the subconscious mind.
2. Most of our beliefs form as children before we develop the ability to analyse and reject them.
3. It leads to the formation of self-limiting beliefs.

Lesson #13: Identify the beliefs holding you back

"Change your thoughts, and you change your world" Norman Vincent Peale

We have established that your perceptions of reality form your beliefs. These are not necessarily accurate representations, leading to false limiting beliefs that were downloaded into your subconscious mind before you could analyse and reject them. The result is that many of us are going through life with a mindset that is not in our best interest and the worst part is you may not even be aware that anything is wrong. You might know that something is holding you back but are unable to pinpoint what it is. The first stage, therefore, is to identify what is holding you back. Only by doing so can you take the necessary action to let them go and replace them with positive beliefs. The process is not easy as these beliefs are stored in the subconscious mind hiding beyond conscious awareness, so it takes some time and effort to understand what it is holding you back. But it is worth it because when you change a limiting belief, your life can change very quickly.

The rest of this chapter explains how you can start communicating with your subconscious mind to see what limiting beliefs you hold. When you learn the language of your subconscious, you can begin to replace old beliefs with new ones.

Identifying limiting beliefs

Start by listening to your inner voice. We talk to ourselves more than we talk to any other person, yet most of us have had limited intimate contact with our voice. Be mindful of what it says. Bear in mind how useful a belief is in serving you. If it doesn't help you move forward, then it's a clear indication that it's a limiting belief. The following are some examples to listen out for which indicate a limiting belief:

1. Making excuses
2. Complaining
3. Having negative thoughts
4. Feeling inferior or incapable
5. Thinking to yourself in limiting and unhelpful ways
6. Jumping to conclusions
7. Feeling fearful
8. Worrying about failure and mistakes
9. Procrastinating
10. Being a perfectionist

It can help to think back to times when you tried to achieve something but weren't successful. Think of specific examples and use the list above to help identify if a limiting belief was holding you back. It can be a challenging exercise to do retrospectively so in the future, whenever you struggle with something, try to think of the reasons why. Say the following question to yourself "I can't achieve this because…" and without giving it too much thought, say the first thing that comes to mind. The reason for this is you are trying to access your subconscious mind rather than giving your conscious mind time to think. Keep repeating this process until you can't come up with any more answers. If you struggle to answer the questions, ask yourself the following questions to help bring the limiting belief into your conscious awareness:

1. What resistance am I feeling when I think about achieving this?
2. What is holding me back from overcoming challenges?
3. What am I saying to myself to stop me from doing what is required?
4. What excuses am I making?
5. What am I complaining about or blaming others for?
6. Why do I think this is too hard for me to achieve?
7. What assumptions am I making about my inability to achieve this?
8. How am I labelling myself as I work towards this?
9. What negative thoughts do I have while working towards this?
10. What am I expecting to happen as I work towards this?
11. What stories am I telling myself about what I should and shouldn't be doing?
12. What am I scared of?
13. Am I going over the same work trying to make it perfect?
14. Is what I'm doing right now a distraction, preventing me from doing what's essential?

Write down all your answers. If you have come up with a lot of reasons, it can be helpful to score each out of 10 to determine the ones that are holding you back the most. Think about your answers and what insights they might provide about your limiting beliefs. It can also be helpful to think about where your limiting beliefs come from. By understanding how they formed, you can gain an insight into the references and experiences that support the belief so you will be well-positioned to deal with any references you might encounter in the future.

Lesson summary:

1. Raise awareness of your limiting beliefs by listening to and questioning your thoughts.

Lesson #14: Let go of the coconut

"We are all lies waiting for the day when we will break free from our cocoon and become the beautiful truth we waited for" Shannon Alder

To catch a monkey requires setting a trap with a coconut and some bait. You cut a hole in the side of a coconut, empty its contents, and fill it with bait to lure in the monkey. The trap is tied down so the monkey cannot run away with it. When the monkey spots the bait, it will reach inside the trap to grab it. The monkey puts its hand inside the coconut and grabs the fruit, but the size of the hole is such that the monkey can reach in and touch the food but cannot pull both its hand and the food out together. As you approach, the monkey will frantically try to pull it out but can't. All the monkey has to do is let go, and it would keep its freedom. But it doesn't, and it gets captured. It clings to the coconut despite the consequences of being caught. You might think that the monkey is stupid for doing this, but we do exactly the same thing. Our limiting beliefs are like the coconut. We cling onto them despite the negative consequences they have on our lives. They keep us trapped, and if we just let go, then we'd be free.

Let go of your limiting beliefs

Once you've identified your limiting beliefs, you can begin the process of letting them go. You have a choice to make, continue to hold these beliefs and not progress or let them go and adopt new beliefs that will transform you. But the choice is not always an easy one to make because many references and experiences form our limiting beliefs. The references usually have a significant amount of emotional investment behind them. Emotion creates a barrier to change; therefore, you must work hard to convince yourself that the value of letting the belief go is greater than holding onto it.

Change belief = Value of letting go of a belief > value of holding onto a belief

Even a temporary suspension of a limiting belief is enough to unblock the mind and explore outside the boundaries of the limiting belief. Given a choice, most will want to make the change, but will struggle to convince their subconscious mind that it's the right thing to do. We will look at the value of letting go of a limiting belief versus the value of holding onto it. Hopefully, we can build a strong enough case that there's more value in letting go and start to convince your subconscious that it's the right thing to do.

What is the value of holding on to this belief?

There is only one reason you're holding onto this belief, and that is the misplaced perception that it is keeping you safe or protecting you from loss. Your brain is constantly scanning your environment for threats to your survival. If you perceive something as a threat, it becomes a belief that you consider to be true. For example, you might say to yourself, *"I can't start a business because it's too risky"*. If you say this once, and listen to it, you'll remain in the same familiar situation you've always been in and feel safe. Your subconscious will say, *"We stay safe when we decide not to start a business"*, and so you decide not to act. This mechanism was great when there were genuine threats but starting a business is not a real threat. It is only something your brain perceives as a threat. If it has been your dream to have your own business, but your beliefs are stopping you from taking the plunge, then clearly this can create suffering. Acknowledge that this belief is trying to protect you from potential pain but that in this situation, it is misguided. So, thank it and let it go.

What is the value of letting go of this belief?

The second part of the equation is thinking about the value of letting go of the belief. If you hold onto your limiting beliefs, think about the consequences: what will you not achieve, who will you not become, what regrets might you have? Associate as much pain as you can for holding onto this belief to provide more motivation to make a positive change in your life. Conversely, think about the potential consequences of adopting a new belief. How will your life change for the better? What will you achieve? The more advantages you can think of, the more motivation you will have to change your belief systems.

Lesson summary:

1. Like the trapped monkey, we cling to limiting beliefs despite the negative consequences they have on our lives.
2. Beliefs are built on many references and experiences, which have a significant amount of emotional investment behind them.
3. This creates a substantial barrier to change therefore you must convince your subconscious that the value of letting them go is greater than holding onto them.

Lesson #15: You are the product of your dominating thoughts

"The spirit of the individual is determined by his dominating thought habits" Bruce Lee

What you focus on, you create more of. The more you think a particular thought, the more neural networks are formed in the brain to support that thought. Likewise, when you stop using a network, it disappears. It means you are capable of physically 'rewiring' yourself. Take power from the fact that real changes are occurring in your brain when you change your mindset. By now, you should have hopefully convinced yourself that the value of letting go of your limiting beliefs is greater than holding onto them and you have started the process of letting them go. The next step is to replace these beliefs with empowering ones.

Adopt new empowering beliefs

Every thought, word, or action you make is either reinforcing deep-set beliefs or creating new beliefs. Choose thoughts, words, and actions that leave impressions on your subconscious mind, so it continually steers you in the direction you want. If your subconscious is stopping you from progressing towards success, you need to learn how to influence it to do what you want.

Belief transformation comes down to building reliable references that help support your new belief. To do this, you need to speak the same language as your subconscious, and that language is emotion and repetition. Strong emotions form strong references and repetition validates those references, making you believe them. When you think about your new beliefs, try to associate them with positive emotions. To do this, think of a time when you felt a strong positive feeling every time you think about your new belief. Through repetition of this process, you will eventually get through to your subconscious. The more references you can collect, the stronger your new belief will become, which will subsequently weaken your old limiting belief. By building a body of evidence in favour of your new belief and against your old belief, you will transform yourself.

Use the limiting beliefs you identified earlier in the chapter to create new beliefs which are the exact opposite. Also, add a statement to help you overcome your false belief. To illustrate the process, let's revisit the earlier examples and see how these beliefs are transformed into positive beliefs:

1. Change 'I'm not ready' to 'I am ready now and will continue to learn and grow along the way'. You won't know everything you'll need before you start but have confidence that you will learn what you require along the way. Don't miss out on what could be the greatest experience of your life because you feel you're not ready. It's a misunderstanding of the word ready. It doesn't mean you've removed all uncertainty; it means you've prepared well, and now it's time to act.

2. Change 'I don't know how' to 'I don't know everything right now; however, I know what I need to take the first or next step. I have confidence in my ability to find out what I require for the next step'.

3. Change 'It's been done before' to 'I have a unique combination of skills, insights, desires, and experiences, and can bring value to this venture'. If you haven't done it, it hasn't been done. Change your scarcity mindset to one of abundance. There is enough for everyone.

4. Change 'Who am I to try that?' to 'I am entitled to try anything I desire'. If you can envisage a dream, you can achieve it.

5. Change 'It's too late' to 'The time is right for me now'. We all have this moment right here and now.

6. Change 'I'm not good enough' to 'I am capable of limitless things'. You won't know all there is to know or have all the tools you need, but you are enough to begin right now.

7. Change 'I don't have time' to 'I respect my dreams enough to give them the time they deserve'. We all have the same 24 hours in a day, become aware of

how you spend yours, and respect yourself enough to prioritise part of your day to what's important to you.

8. Change 'I can't be myself, or I'll be judged' to 'I can be myself, and if people judge me, I understand that I will never please everyone'.

9. Change 'I don't need or deserve to be successful' to 'I'm entitled to dream and deserve to be happy and successful'. No one person is more deserving of success. If you're prepared to work for it, it can be yours.

10. Change 'I am scared of rejection' to 'I understand and embrace that rejection is a part of life and I will strive to learn from any rejection I experience'.

Drown yourself in positive beliefs, write them down and say them out loud to yourself regularly. Recall memories that invoke strong emotions when doing so. It will rewire your brain and train it to think differently. When reprogrammed, your subconscious mind will be on the lookout for opportunities that will move you towards success that you wouldn't usually see.

As you start taking action in the direction of success, you will start building up a new database of beliefs that give you more and more confidence. As the evidence in favour of your new belief starts to outweigh your old belief, your mindset will permanently change. As you begin acting in a way that is consistent with your new belief, you will start building up more and more evidence that supports the belief. This process can take some time, so be patient. Before long you'll have plenty of evidence which supports the new belief, and you'll wonder why you ever gave any weight to your old limiting belief. Your new beliefs will drive the change you desire in your life, so the process is worth the effort.

Lesson summary:

1. Your thoughts have the power to make physiological changes in your brain
2. Choose thoughts that support your new belief and use emotion and repetition to get through to your subconscious

2 ATTITUDES

"Nothing can stop the man with the right mental attitude from achieving his goal; nothing on earth can help the man with the wrong mental attitude" Thomas Jefferson

Your attitude is how you respond to the things that happen to you, and it determines your actions towards them. Having the right mental attitude is an essential prerequisite to success. Attitudes can be positive and will help progress you towards success or negative and will hinder your progress. The lessons presented in this chapter are what I aim to live by in my attempt to be a positive person. They are lessons I consider to be essential to sustaining a positive life.

The type of positive person I strive to be is one who can:

- Understand and focus on what I can control and let go of the rest
- Take full responsibility for everything that happens to me
- Adopt a growth mindset where anything is learnable
- See a mistake or failure as an opportunity to learn
- Separate who I am from what happens to me
- Let go of the past
- Be present and live in the moment
- Appreciate what I have
- Adapt to change
- Limit my exposure to negativity

Each one of these attributes should increase your positivity, and we will explore them over the lessons of this chapter.

Lesson #16: Let go of what you can't control

"God, grant me the serenity to accept the things I cannot change, the courage to change the things I can, and wisdom to know the difference" Serenity Prayer, Reinhold Niebuhr

We try our best to control the outcome of events by putting in place detailed plans, thinking about what could go wrong upfront and taking measures to reduce the risk. This need for security and control comes back to your survival instinct. Rather than respond to danger as it appears, we have the mental capacity to forecast risk and plan preventive measures to avoid danger before it occurs. Because of this ability, we tend to think we are in control.

But the truth is, very little is within your direct control. This lesson is about understanding the difference between what is and isn't within your control. When you know what you can control, you can focus on those things knowing that you can affect a change in that area. The list of things within your control is minimal, but this is good because it reduces the things you need to focus on. There is clarity in simplicity. You can control your thoughts, your beliefs, your attitude, and your actions. For everything else, accept you cannot control it.

Thriving out of control

When you realise that very little is really within your control, your instinctive reaction is likely to be anxiety. Your brain will hate feeling out of control. But this can be a positive. When you relinquish control over the things you have no control over, your attachment to particular outcomes will disappear. This is a good thing because it is attachment to things and outcomes that cause pain and suffering when things don't turn out as expected. Now, if something unexpected happens, you can easily accept the new direction and try again. You feel no suffering over the sudden change because you know you never had control over the outcome. You simply do the best you can, aim high, but without expecting full control over the outcome.

When you feel negative emotions, ask yourself whether there is anything within your control, you can do to help. If the answer is no, accept it and let it go. A wise person knows what they can control and lets go of the rest.

Lesson summary:

1. You can only directly control your thoughts, beliefs, attitudes, and actions.
2. When you relinquish control of the things you can't control, your attachment to particular outcomes will disappear.
3. Do something to change the things we can control; accept the things we cannot control and let them go.

Lesson #17: Between stimulus and response is the freedom to choose

"The last of the human freedoms is to choose one's attitude in any given set of circumstances" Viktor Frankl

We allow so many things that are outside our control to affect us. We get stressed or annoyed when sitting in traffic or if a flight is delayed. Any number of things can happen during a day that can affect our mood. Most of those things you won't be able to control. They will happen whatever you do. You can't change that. There is an important lesson to help you deal with those things and hand the control back to you. You can't always control the situation, but you can control how you respond to the things that happen to you.

The story of Viktor Frankl best illustrates the power to control how you respond to a given set of circumstances. Viktor was a Jewish psychologist living in Austria when the Nazis took power. Frankl was a doctor of neurology in a hospital for mentally ill Jewish children and feeling a sense of duty towards them, decided to stay in Nazi-occupied Austria. Unfortunately, he paid the price for this. Frankl and his family were captured and sent to concentration camps. When prisoner, Frankl observed that there were differences between those who lived and those who died, despite facing the same horrific conditions. The difference was in the meaning and purpose they had for living. In his book, *Man's Search for Meaning,* he writes *"Everything can be taken from a man but one thing: the last of the human freedoms – to choose one's attitudes in any given set of circumstances, to choose one's own way".* It became all too apparent to Frankl when his Nazi captures tortured him; they could do whatever they wanted to his body, but they couldn't destroy his mind unless he let them. Amazingly, Frankl survived three years in multiple concentration camps. When he was released, he learned that the Nazis had murdered most of his family, including his pregnant wife. Despite this unbelievable despair, he found purpose in spreading his message and soon after published his book *Man's Search for Meaning* which went on to sell over 10 million copies.

As Frankl observed, the last of the human freedoms is to choose your attitude. However bad your circumstances, you have full control over how you respond towards them. Two people can experience the same events, but it is their attitude that will determine how they respond. Road rage is an excellent example of this. One driver could respond aggressively when another car cuts them up, beeping their horn and swearing at the driver as if it were a personal attack on them. Responding in this way, the driver will be angry and agitated, which will have a negative impact on the rest of their day. Another person, when faced with the same situation, could realise that it is was an honest mistake which has led to a minor inconvenience, delaying them by a few seconds and not respond at all. That person continues with the rest of their day as if nothing had happened to them. There are things in life you have no control over, like the other car pulling out in front of you, but you always have control over how you respond. When you realise this, you have mastery over yourself, and you can control your life. You can choose to respond in a manner that will best serve you. Like the calm driver who chose not to react aggressively, you move on with your day unaffected.

When a particular situation arises, carefully select how you want to respond based on your values and your desired outcomes. If you start to think the problem is out there, stop because that's the problem. Start with you. Now, whenever I'm faced with a difficult or potentially stressful situation, I remind myself that I have complete control over how I respond to it. I experience much less stress and feel more in control because of this way of thinking.

Lesson summary:

1. Don't look to control external things; look to control your response towards them.
2. Carefully select how you want to respond based on the outcome you would like.

Lesson #18: Take full responsibility for everything that happens to you

"We are all self-made men and women, but only the successful take credit for it" Darren Hardy

In life, we are faced with choices every day. Over time, the choices we make, however small and seemingly insignificant, determine the results we get. When faced with the decision to go to the gym or watch another episode of your favourite show on Netflix, whichever path you take, you must live with the consequences. Choose to watch 5 hours of TV every night, and you're the one who has to live with the result of that. Choose to exercise, eat well, and learn new things, and you also live with the consequences. Wherever you are in life right now, is a result of the choices you have made up to this point. Whether you consider yourself to be a success or a failure, it's all your fault. The best news about this is your future is entirely in your own hands. That is, provided you accept full responsibility for the choices you make.

There are two primary mindsets when thinking about our results:

1. Don't take responsibility

Choices ➡ Decision ➡ Results

⬆

Believe others and external factors decide
so results are not within our control

Most people fail to take full responsibility for their actions. They blame other people or things, making endless excuses and complaints, directing all their judgement towards the person or reason they perceive to be responsible. All the things we do when we fail to accept responsibility imply that we have no control over our situation. And when you feel you don't have control, you won't take any action to change your situation and end up trapped. If you continue to blame, make excuses, or judge someone or something else for an element you don't like about your life, you remain out of control.

2. Take responsibility

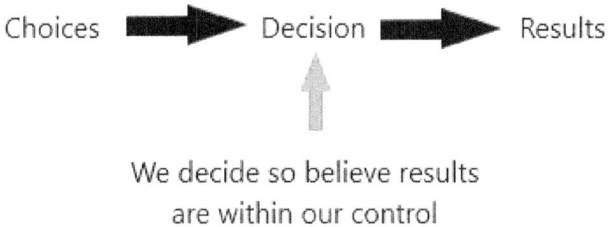

Choices ➡ Decision ➡ Results

We decide so believe results
are within our control

We understand that we are entirely free to decide which option we take when faced with a choice. As such, we are in control of the results we achieve. We take responsibility for our own actions, knowing that they lead to the results we get. When you take 100% responsibility for everything you experience, you own all of your choices entirely. You hold the power. Everything is up to you. You are saying that whatever happens to you, good or bad, is completely down to you. When you take responsibility, you replace negative emotions such as anger and frustration towards other people and situations with positive emotions such as clarity, calmness, and focus. When you feel negative emotions rising in you, say to yourself "I alone am responsible for my thoughts and actions". This empowering attitude will revolutionise your life. Luck, circumstances, or the right situation aren't what matters. What matters is you take on 100% responsibility, and whatever happens, you're still 100% in control of you.

You're probably reading this thinking you take responsibility, but when you think about it, you'll most likely find some finger-pointing, blaming, and expecting someone else to solve your problems. The next time something goes wrong at work, ask yourself whether there was anything you could have done to prevent the situation. Make this your first thought rather than thinking who can I blame for this. If you ever blame the traffic because you're late or blame your bad mood because of something your child, spouse, or co-worker did, you're not taking 100% responsibility. Blaming your results on something external is not accepting full responsibility. You and you alone are responsible for your actions.

If you look at your life right now, realise that this is what your life will continue to be like unless you take responsibility for it and do something about it. Unless *you* change, nothing will change. No one else will change it for you. So, start accepting more and more responsibility. Take responsibility for your job; do more than the minimum required to get by. Take responsibility for your finances, learn how to manage your own money. Take responsibility for your health and fitness. Learn how to eat well rather than leaving it to the doctor to fix you. Take responsibility for your relationships. Too many people are looking for someone else to be responsible for these crucial areas of your life. Stand up and take responsibility for every aspect of your life. It's your life, own it. Decide today to take complete control of your thoughts, feelings, and actions. You become a much more effective, positive, and happy person in everything you do when you accept responsibility for your own life. Your future is in your hands but only if you take responsibility for it and act today.

Lesson summary:

1. Your results are the product of the choices you make
2. Fail to accept responsibility, and you have no control over your results.
3. Take on more responsibility in every area of your life to have greater control over your results.

Lesson #19: Everything is learnable

"If you are not willing to learn, no one can help you. If you are determined to learn, no one can stop you" Zig Ziglar

Your best asset is your ability to learn. The skills and knowledge you acquire over your lifetime will earn you more than anything else. Therefore, what you decide to learn will dramatically shape your life. Most go through school and work and learn just enough to get by. After that, they stop learning, making little or no effort to upgrade their knowledge or skills. They coast. But the only direction you can coast is downhill.

The choice to continue or stop learning new knowledge and skills is ultimately yours to make. If there's one lesson in this book that will have the most significant impact on your attitude, it's this one: everything is learnable. If you want more money, learn how to do this. If you want to live a happier life, learn how to do this. If you want to be more confident, learn how to do this. Everything is learnable. Most don't realise this. They think they can't do certain things and never will so don't put in the time and effort required to develop the skill. As such, it becomes self-fulfilling and reinforces their belief. They look at others who have achieved extraordinary things and tell themselves that they've had more luck than us or are more naturally talented. This is not the case.

Growth vs fixed mindset

As children, we are praised and criticised for the things we do. As such, we see ourselves as good or bad at something depending on the feedback we receive, and this develops the attitudes we hold about our abilities. There are two opposing attitudes you can have towards your skills:

1. They are fixed and will never change - a fixed mindset
2. They are not set and, with effort, can be developed - a growth mindset

With a fixed mindset, you see your abilities as being fixed traits. The consequences of thinking this way are:

1. You believe that natural talent alone leads to success and that talent or skills are something we are born with and have no control over. And for those lucky few talented people, they're just naturally gifted. You believe that because you don't have the skills and talents required for something, you'll never have those skills. You decide because you weren't born with enough talent, there's nothing more you can do so you quit. You remain fixed about your abilities, and close the door to progress.

2. You tie your identity to the fixed trait. For the things you consider yourself to be good at, when something happens to contradict it, you believe you're a failure. For example, imagine a person who excels playing golf as a young child and aspires to play professionally. When it doesn't work out, and they don't play professionally, they consider themselves a failure. To them, they are a golfer, that is their identity. So, when told they are not good enough, it shatters their whole world. In saying they are not a good enough golfer; they hear this as they are not a good enough person.

With a growth mindset, you believe that your talents are not fixed and can be developed. You know that the effort you put in determines your success. So, you just put in more time and effort if you want to develop a talent. If you have a setback, it just means you haven't worked hard enough, and with more work, you'll achieve what you are trying for.

So, when plan A doesn't work out, you are flexible enough to turn to plan B instead of thinking you're a failure and quitting. Michael Jordan failed to make his high school basketball team, and his coach told him he wasn't tall enough. So many would have stopped playing, but if you have a growth mindset, you stick with it because you know that practice will make you better. Think of all the potential sportspeople, artists, actors, and entrepreneurs who quit before they put in the effort to develop their talents. You can learn and develop any ability through work and effort, provided you have a growth mindset.

<u>Change from fixed to growth</u>

If you have a fixed mindset, train yourself to have a growth mindset by recognising fixed mindset thoughts when they arise, then decide if you want to put the work in to develop that skill or talent. If you do, then put in more work. It is thought that to become an expert at something, you must spend 10,000 hours working on it. This is five years, working 40-hour weeks. No one is born excellent or becomes excellent by accident; you must decide to be and make a commitment to work at it. Realise you can learn anything you desire with enough effort and work and you unlock the key to unlimited personal and professional development. Then the rest will look at you as one of the 'lucky' ones who are 'naturally' talented at what you do.

Lesson summary:

1. Your ability to learn can be your best asset
2. With a fixed mindset, you see your abilities as fixed and so cannot be developed.

3. With a growth mindset, you believe your abilities are not fixed and can be developed with enough effort.

Lesson #20: Redefine failure

"I failed my way to success" Thomas Edison

As young children, we take failure in our stride. When learning to walk and talk, we fail over and over again, but eventually one day, we take our first step and speak our first word. Without those failures, we would never succeed. It is a natural part of the learning process. When starting something new, we will be clumsy and make mistakes. You can't expect to do something for the first time and be where you want to be instantly. As we grow up, we learn that failure is a negative thing that we must avoid at all costs. Performance is assessed in every aspect of a child's life. We get praised for good performance at school, at home, in sports teams, and criticised for failing. We are continuously scored, ranked, and judged according to ability. Our culture is one where failure is judged to be a weak character trait, and this has a real negative impact into our adult lives where, as soon as we step out of our comfort zones, failure is inevitable. Fearing failure and judgment, we structure our lives in a way that means we never challenge our self. You tell yourself that because you're not failing, you're doing well in life. The reality is, if you're not failing, you're not pushing yourself, and you're not progressing. You're standing still and settling for what's comfortable.

Redefine failure

When working on the light bulb, a reporter asked Thomas Edison *"How does it feel to fail 10,000 times?"* Edison replied, *"I have not failed 10,000 times; I have successfully found 10,000 ways which will not work"*. With this kind of mindset, you never fail, you just find ways that don't work. The more ways you can find that don't work, the closer you get to finding the way that does work.

Everybody wants to jump to the end of the race but what people don't understand about success is that you have to pay the price. Imagine the route from where you are now to where you want to be but at various points along that route lies hundreds of failures. Think of them as toll booths and you must pay the fee to pass through them. For those unwilling to pay the price, they take failure as an endpoint, and it puts an unnecessary end to their progress.

Unsuccessful people try a few new things, encounter some failure, and think it's the end so go back to what they were doing before. This is true failure. Instead of seeing failure as something to fear, redefine the concept from a negative to a positive. Change your mindset, so instead of seeing failure as an endpoint, it is just a checkpoint along the route to your dream life. To reach the end destination, you have to pass through these failures. There is no way around them. Use the toll booths as signposts, pointing the way for you. And when you do pass through them, you learn something valuable on which your ultimate success will depend.

Success, therefore, is a numbers game and one in which you should fail fast and fail often. Kevin Hart had 3,607 rejections before making it as an actor. Expect to fail and fall short many times before you achieve your goals. Therefore, rather than seeing failure as something to fear, it should be embraced and even sought after. Imagine you must fail 3,607 times before you reach your dreams, the quicker you fail, the faster you get there. The game is to keep showing up despite repeated failure. You can't control the failure, but you can control whether you keep showing up. The person who wins is the person who shows up one more time than the person who just quit. You decide which person you want to be.

Aim to fail daily. Ask yourself at the end of the day, *"Did I fail today?"* If the answer is no, then you didn't challenge yourself enough. And when you do fail, be proud that you pushed yourself beyond your current capabilities and learnt something new. Because next time you encounter the same challenge, the knowledge you gained will mean you're able to overcome it.

Famous failures

The list of famous failures is vast, mostly since every famous person has gone through failure to get to where they are. But in case you have any doubts that failure is a prerequisite to success, here are a few of my favourite famous failures:

1. He was cut from his high school basketball team. He went home from school that day, locked himself in his room, and cried. Perhaps his most famous quote is *"I've lost almost 300 games, 26 times I've been trusted to take the game-winning shot and missed. I've failed over*

    and over and over again in my life, and that is why I succeed" – Michael Jordan

2. He wasn't able to speak until he was almost four years old and his teachers said *"He would never amount to much"* – Albert Einstein

3. She was demoted from her job as a news anchor because she *"Wasn't fit for television"* – Oprah Winfrey

4. He was fired from a newspaper for *"Lacking imagination"* and *"Having no original ideas"* – Walt Disney

5. At age 11, he was cut from his team after being diagnosed with a growth hormone deficiency, which made him smaller in stature than most kids his age – Lionel Messi

6. A high school dropout, whose personal struggles with drugs and poverty culminated in an unsuccessful suicide attempt – Eminem

7. Rejected by Decca recording studios who said *"We don't like their sound… they have no future in show business"* – The Beatles

Lesson summary:

1. We fear failure, so we structure our lives to avoid it and never push ourselves.

2. Redefine failure from a negative to a positive and think of it as something you must pass through on your way to success.

Lesson #21: Separate who you are from what happens to you

"Your present circumstances don't determine where you can go; they merely determine where you start" Nido Qubein

The first lesson in the chapter was how to let go of what you can't control. And something that we have no control over is the past. But more than anything, it's something we can struggle to accept and let go. Over the next two lessons, I will share with you a technique I have found useful for doing that. I realised that unless I made an effort to let go, my past would continue to affect my future. So many of us allow our past to affect the present and future, and for what? We can't change what has already gone. Thinking about it only prolongs our suffering. The best we can do is accept it and not allow it to affect our present or future.

People like to view their past as being who they are. They think the things they've done or not done define them and connect their identity to those events. So, when they have terrible experiences, they use that to define them. Not only that, but when bad things happen to you, you think you're a bad person, or there's something wrong with you. But this is not the case. Life is simply random, and bad things happen to good people. By separating your identity from the things that happen to you, when bad things happen, you don't associate these with your identity and allow them to limit who you can become. Just accept that bad stuff will happen, and it is not a reflection of your character. You are not your past.

Lesson summary:

1. Most struggle to let go of their past because they tie their identity to it, so it is like letting go of a part of themselves.
2. The first step in letting go of the past is to separate who you are from what happens to you.

Lesson #22: Let go of the past

"If you want to fly on the sky, you need to leave the earth. If you want to move forward, you need to let go the past that drags you down" Amit Ray

The next stage of letting go is acceptance and forgiveness. If we can accept what we can't control, then the first part is easy. The past is something that is beyond our control and nothing we can do will change that fact. If we can forgive ourselves and others, we can finally let go of our suffering. We can all feel bogged down by the weight of past mistakes or regret things we've done or neglected. We can all feel anger and sadness about the unfair and unjust things that have happened to us. If you can relate to this, you're not alone, we all experience bad things sometimes which aren't our fault. But if you continue to play these things over in your head, you will continue to suffer, and your past will continue to affect your future. You do not have to be the victim anymore; you can let it go and move on with your life. You survived whatever it was and are now more resilient because of it.

End the suffering

To end the suffering, it comes down to forgiveness. The type of forgiveness depends on the source of pain:

1. Forgive yourself for the mistakes you've made in the past. Nothing can change what has happened, but you don't deserve to serve a self-imposed life sentence to atone for the wrong you have done or bad choices you've made in the past. Most people will try to make the best decision with the information available at the time. There's a high chance that we've all done or said things we regret. But you must forgive yourself to let go.

2. Forgive others that have wronged you. The strange thing is, when you do this, you liberate yourself, not them. Having strong negative feelings towards someone else impacts you more than it does them. You're the one who is having negative thoughts, which will affect your mood and the quality of your life. A quote by Ann Larders sums it up well: *"Hanging onto resentment is letting someone you despise live rent-free in your head"*. If you decide to forgive that person, you're permitting yourself not to be bothered by them anymore. You free your mind up for more positive thoughts and can put an end to your suffering.

Let it go

Whatever has happened in your past, you can choose the power over your life it has. It is a very liberating feeling because it means whatever has come before should not affect your ability to make the right decisions for your future. Your past will only have a grip on your present if you let it. It is the choices you make in the present moment that will determine your future, not those you've already made. Your job is not to let past actions interfere too much with the present. If you have the mindset that "I've neglected my health in the past so will neglect it again in the future" your past is interfering too much with your future. Your past performance does not determine your future. Accept that you can't change events that have happened, but you do have complete autonomy over your choices in the present moment.

- You can succeed in business even if you failed before
- You can get in shape even if you have been overweight
- You can enjoy a happy relationship even if your last partner cheated on you
- You can experience abundance even if you grew up poor
- You can be a good parent even if your own weren't
- You can be happy even if you have experienced pain
- You can get your dream job even if you were fired from your previous one
- You can get your degree even if you've neglected your education in the past
- You can learn to trust again even if others have betrayed you

When you let go of your past, you create space for a clean start. From this point onwards, your choices and actions in the present moment will define your future. Decide to learn from your past and apply it to the present so you can live the life you want. Use this lesson to make peace with your past, accept that life is random, and what happens to you does not define you. The present moment in your life is a new beginning. From this point forward, everything you want is possible and available to you.

Lesson summary:

1. Forgive yourself and those who have wronged you in the past.
2. Let go of the past by focusing on the present moment.

Lesson #23: Live rich today

"Do not set aside your happiness. Do not wait to be happy in the future. The best time to be happy is always now" Roy Bennett

We all want success in our lives. Despite this, a lot of people get it wrong and chase things they think will bring them success only to find out when they get there, that they're no happier. It turns out that there's a big divide between what we think will bring us success and what does. Success is not the prize for a lifetime's worth of sacrifices. It is not an end goal that you have to wait decades for. In this lesson, you will see that success is a lifestyle that can be lived right now.

What we think success is – The Ladder Life

For a long time, I followed the approach that I'll be happy when I reach the next level of life. I saw life as a sequential path of the actions you should complete that will lead you to success. You get good grades at school, then get your degree and a good job, marry the perfect partner, buy a house, have kids, get promoted, earn more money, get a bigger house, a better car, and live happily ever after. And only after you've walked the entire path will you find success. Even the saying "happily ever after" implies you must first find something to be happy. You think you'll be satisfied when you make more money, lose weight, fall in love, move to a new house or start a new job. With this never-ending desire, we're continuously searching for the next thing to make us happy. You might get temporary pleasure from these things, but it is short-lived. Before long, you'll be back to saying, "I'll be happy when I get on the next rung of the ladder". Then when you get there, you're still not happy because you have the next rung to climb.

When we focus on what we don't have, we live as if something is missing and so can't experience success in the present moment. We have it backwards. Success is not a destination; it's the journey.

What actually brings us success

There is a different approach and one which gives control back to you. Rather than focus on your desired outcome and put off success until you reach it, you simply focus on and enjoy the present moment and live rich today.

I have lived the ladder life and always strived to get onto the next rung on the ladder. But in this constant search for more and more, I felt as though I was becoming less. I was living mostly in my head, suffering over past experiences, and worrying about an uncertain future. When you're so focused on these things in your mind, you stop engaging with the world in the present moment. And your life goes by without you ever really living. It's like the film *Click* where Adam Sandler's character acquires a remote that allows him to fast forward through unpleasant and dull parts of his life. He uses the remote to skip ahead to his promotion a year into the future and realises that he's missed some crucial parts of his life. The remote starts to learn his preferences and skips forward to his next promotion when he becomes CEO of his company. It is ten years in the future where he is now obese, and his wife has left him. The remote keeps skipping years of his life, and he misses his children grow up and the death of his father. Always living in your head, focusing on the past and future is the same. Your life flashes by, and you never take the time to enjoy the journey. I have realised that life is not about climbing to the top of the ladder. For me, it's about enjoying the present moment and appreciating what I have. These are the subjects of the next two lessons.

Lesson summary:

1. Most see success as an endpoint, and it only comes after you reach the next level of life.
2. We have it backwards; success is not an endpoint, it's the journey.

Lesson #24: Be present

"In today's rush, we all think too much, seek too much, want too much, and forget about the joy of just being" Eckhart Tolle

The past is a record of moments that we have no control over, and which cannot be changed. The future is something we try our best to predict, but there are infinite possible outcomes. So when your thoughts get caught in one of them, you're just imagining something that has almost no chance of occurring. Unfortunately for you, your brain is sold on the idea that the next moment is more important than the one you're in. And the moment that has already passed is more familiar and therefore more comfortable. These biases of the brain are what make it easy to dwell on the past or prepare for an imagined future that is unlikely to occur.

When we're focused on the past or the future, we're living in our thoughts, not in reality. Getting caught up in your head is a dangerous place to be because we neglect to live in the present moment. It can feel as though you have constant brain fog, time passes by quickly, and you never experience true living. Life can only happen to us in the present moment. It's the only moment we can ever really experience. To become aware of the beauty of life unfolding around you, you need to get out of your head and into the present moment. Success is when you're in the moment and doing things you love with people you care about.

Live in the present and be happy today with what you do. Focus on the thoughts and ideas that bring you happiness today. Be present and satisfied with where you're at while exploring new things and intentionally working towards something more. It's not either-or. Remember, there's always a future, but there is only one present.

When you think about something that causes you pain and suffering, that thought is almost always anchored in the past or future. While all emotions are felt in the present, negative emotions tend to have an anchor in the past or future. Examples of emotions anchored in the past include regret, embarrassment, guilt, shame, grief, envy, annoyance, and judgement. Examples of those rooted in the future include stress, anxiety, fear, worry, helplessness. To make a judgement, you compare a current observation with one you've made in the past. To be anxious, you need to think about the future and anticipate that it will be worse than the present. To be bored, you long for something other than what's happening in the present. To be ashamed, you need to recreate a moment that no longer exists. Notice that for the thoughts that cause you suffering, very few of the emotions associated with them have anything to do with the present moment.

Almost all feelings anchored in the present moment are positive. These include emotional states such as calm, affection, empathy, love, courage, pride, satisfaction, trust, contentment, relaxation, and relief. Therefore, if we can work to be more focused on the present, we can experience more positive emotional states.

Stay entirely focused on the present moment

So, what can we do to keep us in the present moment? Try the following exercise. Sit down and make yourself comfortable. Close your eyes for a few seconds. Now open your eyes again and look to observe everything around you. Use all your senses to take in as much information as you can. Do this for about 10 seconds then close your eyes again. Describe to yourself in detail what you saw, heard, and felt. Be factual, and don't let your thoughts interrupt. If you do this correctly, it will take you several minutes to describe what you saw in just a few seconds. Observing something requires simple awareness but describing it introduces much lengthier thought processes. Limit your thoughts to what you've just seen in the present moment.

Due to your brain's ability to only focus on one thought at a time, if you can focus on your immediate surroundings, it leaves no room for past or future thoughts. It means all the negative emotions anchored to them also disappear, so your thoughts are calmer. When you tune into the present moment, you accept it as it is. You don't compare it or judge it to the past or try to predict how it could be different in the future. It's peaceful, and there's no drama. It is simply stating what you see.

What I have just explained to you is meditation. For years, I didn't understand meditation, and it wasn't until I read it in the way described above, that I realised what it was all about. It made sense all of a sudden, so I tried it. And it worked. It helps me to become anchored in the present moment and has a calming effect. If you can't relate to any of the above, try the following instead:

1. Be curious and set out each day to find out something new. Monitor everything and take as much in as possible. Give yourself a reason to be alert to your surroundings and the present moment. It also helps to remove autopilot. I tried this on my morning commute and when sat in traffic, noticed hundreds of mistletoe plants hanging from some trees which I'd never noticed before. There is so much around us that we are blind to because we live on autopilot. When you're in the present moment, you see so much more.

2. On autopilot, your days pass without a single minute of stillness. Whenever you feel your mind racing or your day rushing passed, just stop. Tell yourself that you're not going back to life until you observe ten things around you.

3. Use a totem. In the film *Inception*, a totem is used to distinguish between a dream and being awake. You can do the same thing to remind you that it's time to be aware, to come off autopilot. It must be something odd enough to serve as a reminder when you see it. And when you do, stop everything, and raise your awareness. Get fully absorbed in the present moment to become entirely free of your thoughts.

4. Remove all devices that tell the time and escape from time once a day if you can.

5. Do only one thing at a time. Don't watch TV while you eat dinner. Whatever you do, give it your undivided attention.

Every stressful or unhappy thought exists outside of the here and now while every observation in the present moment takes you to a peaceful place. Every time you examine your thoughts, you will notice that whatever you're upset about is rooted in a past experience you cannot change or a future that may turn out to be completely different. Let the past and future go and do your best with whatever you're doing in the present moment. This moment is all you have. Live in it fully, and the rest will take care of itself. You're alive now, in this moment. There will never be any other time.

Now that you have the tools you need; will you stay in your head or will you spend every day experiencing each moment to the fullest? Will you waste time regretting the days that have past or worrying about days yet to come or will you spend every day experiencing life? Life is now. In the present. Live it.

Lesson summary:

1. Negative emotions are anchored to the past and future; positive emotions are rooted in the present
2. To experience more positive emotions, get out of your head, away from the past and future, and into the present
3. The present moment is all there is, live in it

Lesson #25: Focus on and appreciate what you have

"Gratitude unlocks the fullness of life. It turns what we have into enough, and more. It turns denial into acceptance, chaos into order, confusion to clarity. It can turn a meal into a feast, a house into a home, a stranger into a friend. Gratitude makes sense of our past, brings peace for today, and creates a vision for tomorrow"
Melody Beattie

Society is designed to make you focus on what you don't have in an attempt to make you want the thing you're missing. It sells you the idea of something you don't have to make you think you must have it. You might think you need the latest phone, a new car, or your own house. But when you focus on what you don't have, you forget all the great things that you've already got. For this reason, I define gratitude as concentrating on what you do have rather than on what you don't. The interesting thing is, by focusing on and showing appreciation for the things you do have, it makes it easier to gain the things you don't have. This is because when you start showing genuine appreciation towards the aspects in your life which you're grateful for, the people and things in your world will start responding differently to you.

There are three techniques I use to help me focus on and show appreciation towards the things in my life:

1. <u>The butterfly effect</u>

This exercise requires some thought and effort, but it will transform the way you think about what you've got. Identify something positive in your life. It could be the job you love doing, your partner, your children, or your health. Next, list all the circumstances that made it possible for it to be in your life. You'll often find that when you think back to the events that had to happen, it will seem like a miracle that they did. Perhaps, it was a seemingly insignificant decision. You went out for a drink with your friends and ended up meeting your husband or wife. It could have been something that shattered your world at the time, but without that happening, it wouldn't have led you to where you are today. Your partner might have left you, and at the time, this was the worst possible thing that could have happened, but this led you down a path where you met your current partner which led to having your children that you cherish today. Write down as many of these events or decisions as possible if they played a role in you being where you are today.

The next step is to do the eraser test. With your list of events, imagine you have a magic eraser that can remove that event from time and all the events that resulted from it also disappear from time too. Imagine what your life would look like right now had that chain of events not occurred. Given a choice, would you apply the eraser to that event? Most people would say no, even to the most challenging times in their life because those events made them into the person they are and led them on to the life they have and love today.

When you think about those events, remind yourself that life did go your way. Consider the randomness that brought that positive into your life. When I do this myself, I feel an overwhelming sense of gratitude towards the events of my life, even the toughest moments. Without them, I wouldn't be who I am, doing what I'm doing today. I wouldn't be writing these words, and I wouldn't be living a life I love. Not only does it make me appreciate all the positive things in my life but with this attitude, whatever happens to me, good or bad, I know that it can lead me down a path towards an even greater life in the future.

2. Keep a gratitude log

The second technique is to keep a gratitude log. You simply write down things you appreciate. If you write down one thing each day that you're grateful for, it will completely change your attitude. You will be on the lookout for positives. It will overwhelm anything negative you have to complain about. Each day, you set out with an intention to find the best things in your life, and when you keep this at the front of your mind, it is exactly what you end up finding.

Whatever you appreciate about your life, write it down. One thing each day might sound difficult, but it can be something small, like your afternoon coffee or your dog greeting you after work. Writing about the people in your life you appreciate can transform your relationships. When you find the best in them and show genuine appreciation for them, they respond differently to you, and your relationship flourishes. You might think that the longer you do this, the harder it would be to find things you appreciate. But the opposite is true. By doing this, you start to appreciate more and more as you transform your attitude. You will automatically seek the positive and show your appreciation towards it. The world will respond differently, and your life will flourish.

3. Appreciate being alive

Have you ever thought about the battle you won just to be alive? The odds you've overcome to be here today. You had to beat tens of millions of competitors to become the only one to reach the goal. A goal so small, it is not even as big as the tip of a needle. Yet on this microscopic level, your life's most decisive battle was fought and won. You rose to the top and were victorious. You won the race and defeated all competitors. You made it to your goal, and the life of the most important living person had begun. Your life had begun.

Everything that has ever happened in the history of time has led up to your birth. The events that lead to your parents' meeting, your grandparents' meeting, and so on. Every decision made by your ancestors. Every war or plague across human history. Every event that occurred over the past million years during the evolution of our species. The extinction events across time, including the one that wiped out the dinosaurs. The formation of life on earth and the forming of the planets. Right back to the big bang and whatever was beyond that. Every single event over the history of time has led to you being here today. You have overcome the most staggering odds you will ever have to face. Odds so small you can't comprehend them. You have everything you'll ever need just being alive and no matter what obstacles or difficulties lie in your way, they don't come close to what you've already overcome just being alive. The next time you have a stressful day, remember that the chances of you being alive are so small that it's a miracle you're here. And that in 100 years, you won't be. It has helped me gain perspective on 'life's problems' and appreciate just being alive.

Lesson summary:

1. Gratitude is focussing on what you do have rather than on what you don't have.
2. Think about all the positives in your life and be grateful for the events that made them happen.
3. Write down one thing each day that you're grateful for.
4. Everything that has happened over the history of time has led to you being alive right now.

Lesson #26: Adapt to change

"Change is the only constant in life" Heraclitus

Change is something we all must deal with daily. Some changes are insignificant and have little effect on our lives, others change everything. Change can cause a great deal of suffering for us. We expect things to stay a certain way, and when this doesn't happen, it leads to suffering. The quote at the beginning of the lesson says it well. The only constant in life is change. So, if we expect change in our lives, when it comes, it will lead to much less suffering.

In his book *Solve for Happy,* Mo Gawdat puts forward a simple equation for happiness: happiness is equal to the events of your life minus your expectations of how your life should be. Written out as an equation this is:

Happiness = Events of your life – Expectations

So, if the events of your life exceed your expectations, you're happy. But if you expect something to be a certain way and it doesn't live up to your expectation, you can feel unhappy. We must understand that when expectations are not adequately managed, they can cause a great deal of pain and suffering. William Shakespeare said, "*Expectation is the root of all heartache*" and he was right.

If your happiness depends on the two factors shown in the equation above, then to increase your happiness, there are only two things you can do:

1. Improve the events of your life

    You won't have full control over the events of your life. You can work hard and do all the right things to level up your life, however, this process is not guaranteed or instant, as it could take years to achieve. In the meantime, are you OK with delaying your happiness until that point? You shouldn't be.

2. Decrease your expectations

    We all expect remarkable things and striving to meet high expectations is how humanity progresses. But when this part of the equation is artificially inflated, the events of our lives may not match them. The solution is simple: adjust your expectations. I want to be clear here, although I'm saying lower your expectations, this doesn't mean you shouldn't strive to develop or progress. It's more about aligning your expectations with where you are currently. Don't start up a new business and expect to be a millionaire the next day. It is about having realistic expectations for the stage that you're at. We have full control over this part of the equation. All we need to do is learn how to manage our expectations, and we can balance the happiness equation and live happy today, while you are in the process of working to improve the events of your life. When you do this, whatever life throws at you, you can control your happiness.

Lesson summary:

1. Change can cause a great deal of suffering due to our expectations towards it.
2. Happiness depends on the events of your life and your expectations.
3. The only part we can fully control is our expectations.

Lesson #27: Disconnect from negativity

"You can't litter negativity everywhere and then wonder why you've got a trashy life" Unknown

The final lesson in this chapter is to remove all significant sources of negativity. Those I consider worth discussing include:

1. The News
2. Social media
3. People

The News

If there's one simple thing you can do right now that will increase your positivity and spirit significantly, it's switch off the news. We are wired to seek negativity, and the media take full advantage of this aspect of our nature. They take a handful of the most brutal and shocking events of the day and parade it all over the news. Taking this in day in and day out can give you a distorted view of the world. The stories that make the news are an extremely narrow view of the world, focusing only on what's not working. It's like looking at the world through filtered glasses, and you can only see the worst the world has to offer. Millions of positive things happen that don't get any attention. Remove the filter and take in the whole picture and you'll see that the bad is only a tiny percentage of what goes on in the world.

Social media

There are two main problems with social media:

1. People, including myself, tend to post the highlight reel of their lives on social media. When you see it, your instinctive reaction is to compare yourself to them. If you perceive their life to be better than yours, it will lead to negative feelings. I'm not saying you shouldn't use social media, just take care when using it and acknowledge what you see for what it is, highlights of people's lives.

2. The second issue which can have an impact on your positivity is reading comments from trolls. The term troll describes anybody who posts inflammatory

and negative messages with the intent of provoking an emotional response. It is all too easy for people to post negative things about others behind the safety and anonymity of the keyboard.

When you decide to take radical action to better yourself, you will inevitably be met by criticism from others. Unfortunately, for our prehistoric brain, we seek acceptance from others as this once offered a survival advantage for our ancestors. So, it is not easy to ignore the opinions of others. The only advice I can provide you with is what others think of you has nothing to do with you and everything to do with them. When they disapprove or criticise, what they are really doing is projecting their beliefs of what is right and wrong onto you, then telling you what their conclusion is. For example, when someone can't do something, their perception is often that it can't be done, and they will project this onto you and say you can't do it. Someone who says "you can't" is showing you their limits, not yours. If you ever receive unjustified negative comments online, remember that the person leaving that comment is projecting their beliefs onto you and letting you know what their conclusion is. Don't look outside yourself for approval; the only approval you need is from within. No one can limit you without your permission. Be passionate about your dreams, protect them, and don't let other people interrupt you and tell you that you can't do it.

People

It's said that you are the average of the five people you spend the most time with. If this is the case, wouldn't you want those people to be supportive, encouraging, and positive? Research by Dr David McClelland of Harvard University suggests that as much as 95 per cent of your success or failure in life is from the people you habitually associate with. If you hang around with negative people, your chances of a positive life are dramatically reduced. You can do all the right things, but without the right people around you to hold you to a higher standard, you will struggle to succeed.

Negative people tend to be the ones who have either never achieved anything significant or tried once and failed. Because they can't do it, no one else can. They will want to see you fail to make themselves feel better. Never let a person who has not done what you want to achieve, tell you how to do anything. One of the most expensive things you can do is pay attention to the wrong people. If you can use their opinion to better yourself in some way, then use it but don't worry about pleasing everyone. Don't try to justify yourself as you will be unlikely to change their beliefs and only end up wasting time. Instead, reduce the time you spend with negative people. If you can, cut them out of your life altogether.

You need to construct your social environment and plan which opinions, attitudes, and philosophies you allow into your life. Surround yourself with people you admire. If we are the average of those we spend the most time with, then we become like the people we expose ourselves to. Find people who are already where you want to be. Their positive behaviours and attitudes which have helped them to reach success will rub off on you and increase your chances of achieving the same thing.

To conclude this lesson, turn off the news and get off social media or at least limit your exposure to 30 minutes a day. Besides improving your mental state, it will also free up time you can spend developing yourself and learning new skills. Learn the difference between *the* world and *your* world and only pay attention to *your* world. It's the only thing you can do anything about. Paying too much attention to the negativity that you can't control will only make you feel fearful, frustrated, and cynical. All you have in life is your attention, and where this goes, your life goes. That choice will affect your experience of life. You can choose to focus on the worst of the world, or you can choose to focus on the best of your world, on the things that you can control, and that have a direct impact on your life.

Lesson summary:

1. Remove all sources of negativity from your life starting with the news, negativity online and negative people.
2. Separate *the* world from *your* world and choose to pay attention to the things in your world that you can control and that will have a positive impact.

3 ACTIONS

In the first two chapters, we've focused on the inward-facing attributes of your personality. Your outward-facing actions reflect those attributes. It is ultimately how you act that will determine your success. In the final part of this section, we will explore how we can better control our actions to help us meet our longer-term goals.

Lesson #28: Work to resolve your goal-motive conflict

"Discipline is the bridge between goals and accomplishment" Jim Rohn

Why is it so difficult to act in a way that is in our best interest? There's enough information available to know what's right for us, yet we struggle to act in this way. For example, how many people would like to lose weight or achieve financial independence? We all want these things, and most of us know what we must do to achieve them: eat plenty of fruit and vegetables, get regular exercise, and save for retirement. Yet, despite wanting these things and knowing how to get them, only a small percentage of people achieve them. Why? Self-control. Those who achieve what they desire have developed this skill. For those who face problems with self-control, it almost always involves a conflict between two competing goals. This is known as a goal-motive conflict, where we have a choice between two options:

1. The vague long-term goal with distant rewards
2. The short-term specific goal with clear, immediate rewards

Why do we give in so easily?

We know what is good for us and we set long term goals in line with this. We plan to eat well, exercise and save money but then something comes along which our brains find irresistible, like chocolate, and we give in to temptation. Now we have two conflicting goals, we want to be healthy in the long-term but also want the chocolate in the short-term. Which one usually wins out? The chocolate. Why? Because the rewards of the short-term goal are clear and instant. Given a choice, most of us will take immediate reward over delayed gratification, even if the rewards for delaying are much greater. This is not a surprise when you consider that instant gratification provides an evolutionary advantage. So again, we are challenged by our own nature. We are hardwired to seek pleasure and not what it best for us. Pleasurable experiences often cause an emotionally charged response that overrides our rational, cognitive systems leading to impulsive actions. This is why, despite knowing what is best for us, we often act in a way that is detrimental to our long-term well-being.

<u>It doesn't have to be this way</u>

If important goals are both vague and distant, the key to self-control seems to be finding a way to promote these rewards over immediate and clear rewards. This requires extra work to make the vague, distant goal more immediate and specific.

The two key concepts we will explore in this chapter are discipline and habit. Discipline is the ability to promote vague and distant rewards over immediate and concrete rewards. Habit is making the behaviour automatic. Discipline is not an easy trait to develop; however, there are some valuable lessons we will explore to help you better understand it. The critical thing to remember is that we are only looking to develop enough discipline to sustain behaviour until habit takes over. The hardest part of the process is the start. We need to apply selective discipline at the beginning of a new behaviour long enough for it to become automatic. This is the ultimate goal because when you can make positive behaviours a habit, minimal discipline is required to sustain them. Discipline will get you going; the habit will keep you going. This chapter aims to resolve your goal-motive conflicts and transform you from someone who knows what the right thing is, into someone who does the right thing.

Lesson summary:

1. If you struggle with self-control you likely have a conflict between two goals: one is vague and distant; the other is concrete and immediate.
2. To develop self-control, we must work to promote vague and distant goals over concrete and immediate goals.

Lesson #29: Don't touch that marshmallow

"Strength does not come from physical capacity. It comes from indomitable will" Gandhi

This lesson is about one of the most famous studies on self-control done by Walter Michael. Children were offered a single marshmallow which they could eat straight away, or two marshmallows if they could wait 15 minutes. The children were left in the room with the marshmallow, and their behaviour was observed. One-third of the children ate the marshmallow immediately, another third waited a while then ate it, and the final third were able to wait the full 15 minutes. However, the most significant finding didn't come until years later. The children who participated in the study included Walter's daughter and her friends. As the children grew up, it became apparent that those who hadn't eaten the marshmallow were performing better at school than those who had. Similar experiments found that those able to put off instant rewards (or delay gratification) were, on average, physically healthier, more academic, and financially more stable as adults.

A child's ability to delay gratification correlates with academic and professional success more than any other measure. More than intelligence, more than standardised testing, more than household income, religion, personality, gender – everything. Therefore, the ability to delay gratification is arguably the most crucial attribute for achieving success. This makes sense. If a child does their homework before going out to play, they will perform better at school. Putting off the instant reward of eating a doughnut in favour of the longer-term health benefits will lead to a healthier person. And the individual who can delay the gratification of spending money and instead save and invest it will be financially stable. If you are looking to achieve anything meaningful in life, chances are it will require sacrificing the immediate reward in favour of the longer-term benefits. If you can be that person who is strong enough to put off instant rewards in favour of delayed gratification, you will change your life. It's as simple as that. Although, as we saw in the previous lesson, the immediate goal is not always so easy to turn down. So, delaying gratification perhaps isn't quite that straightforward. In the remaining lessons of this chapter, we will discuss how we can organise our lives to make it slightly easier.

Lesson summary:

1. The ability to delay gratification is arguably the most important attribute for achieving success.

Lesson #30: Willpower is finite

"He who controls others may be powerful, but he who has mastered himself is mightier still" Lao Tzu

A study by Roy Baumeister inspires this lesson. Participants were presented with a plate of radishes and a plate of freshly baked cookies. They were then split into two groups. One group was asked to eat only the radishes, and the other could eat the cookies. Immediately after, participants were given 30 minutes to complete a complicated puzzle. The radish-eaters gave up on the puzzle after about 8 minutes while those who ate the cookies lasted 19 minutes, on average. Those who had to exert willpower by eating the radishes instead of the cookies gave up over twice as fast. The conclusion: people forced to use willpower on one task, are worse at exerting willpower on subsequent tasks. In other words, willpower is finite and can be drained.

We each have a full tank of willpower every day, and once it's been used, we are far more likely to give up on tasks that require willpower. So, willpower is a reservoir of mental strength, and as we go through the day, we encounter things that need willpower, so it is a depleting resource. We must, therefore, manage it and plan things that require willpower accordingly.

For new behaviours you want to adopt, give yourself the best chance by doing it when willpower reserves are highest, early in the day. The easiest way to do this is to wake up early and work on these tasks which require willpower before going to work. You'll be much more likely to complete them than if you left it until after work when your willpower reserves are low. You make it much harder for yourself trying to tackle tasks that require willpower when you've already depleted your reserves. Also, armed with the knowledge that willpower reserves are low later in the day, you can take steps to avoid the triggers for your bad habits as you're much more likely to act them out with low willpower levels.

Lesson summary:

1. Willpower is a finite resource that is drained throughout the day.
2. Plan your day so you do what matters most when you have full willpower reserves.

Lesson #31: Hijack your willpower

"He that can have patience can have what he will" Benjamin Franklin

So, what can we do to put off instant rewards in favour of the longer-term benefits? In this lesson, we will explore three things to develop your ability to delay gratification.

1. Spot your marshmallows

Recognise and record the objects of your gratification. Throughout the day, be aware of your cravings and desires. When these feelings hit, acknowledge them, and write them down. This simple act will raise your awareness and make you more likely to take the right actions. Introduce small tricks to say, "not now". Remind yourself that it is a choice between what your urges and impulses want now, and what you want most in the long term. You control your desires; they don't control you.

2. Out of sight, out of mind

People who have good self-control are better at structuring their lives in a way that does not require willpower. It makes sense given that willpower is a finite resource. People with the best self-control need to use it the least. Don't wish you were a more disciplined person, create a more disciplined environment. Put distance between yourself and the object of your gratification. The children in the marshmallow study who managed to leave it alone covered their eyes or turned away from it. If you've recognised that when you go shopping, you end up spending money on unnecessary clothes, don't go shopping if your goal is to save money.

3. Set upper limits

Set upper limits on the amount of time you spend per day working on tasks that require willpower. Sustainability and effort are inversely related. So, things that need little effort are highly sustainable; however, those that require a lot of effort can quickly lead to burn out. Somewhere in the middle is the sweet spot. What this means is that you should set upper limits on the time you spend working on tasks that require willpower so you can sustain the effort.

The ability to sacrifice short-term desires for longer-term gain means you no longer have to be a slave to your impulses. When you develop the ability to delay gratification, you have true power and control over your destiny. It comes down to this: rule or be ruled.

Lesson summary:

1. Become aware of the objects of your gratification.
2. Create a more disciplined environment by keeping the objects of your desire out of sight.
3. Set upper limits for the time spent on activities requiring willpower.

Lesson #32: Willpower alone is not enough

"In writing, habit seems to be a much stronger force than either willpower or inspiration" John Steinbeck

Discipline will get you started but used alone, it is not enough. You will revert to your old ways if you rely purely on discipline. It is a useful tool in changing your behaviour, but there is something far more dependable in sustaining long term behaviour change – habit. When you have identified a positive change you want to make, use the previous lessons to help you through the first part of that change. Discipline has its place in helping you establish habits. But don't rely purely on discipline to sustain your success. For long term success, you must use the power of habit.

The successful all share one common trait, they all have 'good' habits. A daily routine built on the right habits is what separates them from the rest of us. They aren't superhuman, they've just used selective discipline to develop a few significant habits, one at a time, over time. Their habits take them in the direction of becoming more informed, more knowledgeable, more competent, better skilled, and better prepared. You are what you repeatedly do. Therefore, success isn't a one-off action but a habit you form. The remainder of this chapter will explore how habits form and how, by having a basic understanding of the habit loop, you can form new habits that will put you on the path to success.

Lesson summary:

1. Willpower will support a behaviour change long enough for habit to take over to sustain the change.

Lesson #33: Good habits pay compound interest

"Little by little, a little becomes a lot" Tanzanian Proverb

We often convince ourselves that success requires big action. That we must become a different person overnight, or drastically change something in our day-to-day life to get results. We underestimate the impact that slight changes can have because they make little difference on any given day. However, small improvements to your daily routine can compound into massive results over the years. One small change can lead to another, then another. Maintain momentum long enough and the slight change to your daily routine snowballs into massive results over time.

To demonstrate the power of compounding, consider the following example. I will use money to illustrate how compounding works, but the same effect applies to your skills, knowledge, and success when small daily steps add up over the years. Do you buy a £5 coffee every morning on the way to work? If so, let's consider the long-term cost of that coffee. £5 each working day is £25 a week or £100 a month. Not a massive amount of money. But let's see what the power of compounding can do over time. If invested, and assuming 10% compounded growth, over 40 years you'd have £560,000. It might seem impossible, but this is the power of compounding. The increase is exponential as the interest you earn starts earning interest. The graph shows the typical progress you can expect to see.

Balance (Compounded Yearly)

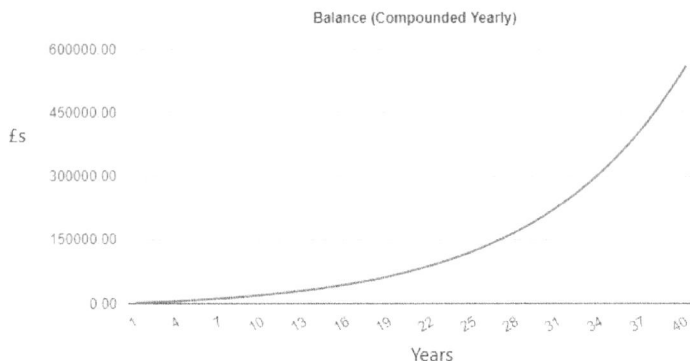

The same compound effect also applies to other areas of your life, including your skills and talents. There is, however, one key ingredient needed for compounding to kick in: time.

People who want to improve their situation will decide to make some changes, but when results don't come quickly, they give up. But it's important to remember that compounding takes time to kick in. Looking at the curve above, it takes about 28 years to reach £150,000, but the next £150,000 only takes about six years.

When you make a small positive change, progress will be slow, and you won't observe the results you want straight away. But keep working at it, and that one slight change to your daily routine will compound into massive results in the long term. Learning a foreign language demonstrates this point well. It takes years to become fluent in the language, and it can seem like you have a mountain to climb when you start learning. Progress will be slow at the beginning as you learn the basics. Most will want to see fast results, and when this doesn't come, they will get disheartened and give up. Instead, realise that the progress curve will look like the one in the graph. Progress initially will be slow, but if you keep your focus on the small daily habit of spending 15 minutes learning, your results will compound over time. What matters most is that your daily habits are putting you on the upward curve to being able to speak the language.

For this reason, your daily habits determine where you will be in 5-, 10- and 20-years' time from now. You become your habits. Make it a habit to spend 15 minutes a day learning a language, and after 20 years this equates to almost 2,000 hours. And all from 15 minutes a day. We like to focus on the end goal of speaking fluently in the shortest possible time when instead, the focus should be on the daily habit required to achieve the outcome. Success is the product of good daily habits and not a once in a lifetime transformation. Get your daily habits right, and your success becomes a question of when, not if.

Lesson summary:

1. Big change doesn't require big action; slight variations to your daily habit compound over the long term to deliver massive results.
2. Compounding takes time so don't expect instant results.

Lesson #34: Remove motivation from the equation

"First forget inspiration. Habit is more dependable. Habit will sustain you whether you're inspired or not. Habit is persistence in practice" Octavia Butler

So, what exactly is a habit? It's behaviour repeated enough times to become automatic. The keyword in that sentence is automatic. Many of the long-term goals you set for yourself require repeating the same actions day-in and day-out, so imagine how much easier it could be to achieve them if these actions became automatic. It shifts the goal-motive conflict in your favour.

Lack of motivation and willpower are key things that stop people from taking action. So, remove them from the equation. By understanding and using the power of habit, you no longer need to rely on motivation to get stuff done. You simply act out the behaviour without much conscious thought or effort.

This lesson explains the basics of habit formation and introduces the components that make a good habit. In the lessons that follow, we will explore practical advice to help you integrate new positive habits into your life and change negative habits that may be preventing you from achieving your goals.

The habit loop

The habit loop consists of three elements: a cue, a routine, and a reward. The cue is anything that triggers the habit. The routine is the action you perform. It could be anything from brushing your teeth to driving or smoking. The reward is the reason you bother completing the activity. Where you gain a reward, the brain catalogues the events that preceded it and creates a feedback loop, so you know to repeat the behaviour in the future when you next encounter the cue. The habit loop will only operate when there is a craving for the reward that drives the loop. If no craving exists for the reward, the habit will not form.

The Habit Loop

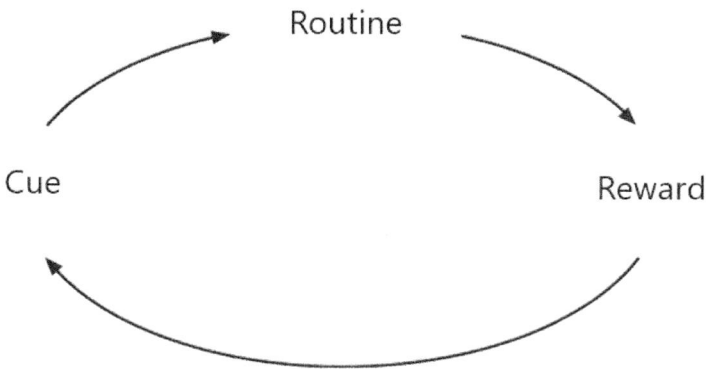

Routine

Cue

Reward

To illustrate how the habit loop works, consider nail-biting as an example. At some point, the individual was in a mental state which led to nail-biting. This state could be stressed, anxious, or bored. The first time they felt this way, they were presented with a problem – feeling a negative emotion. The first time we face an issue in which we don't have the solution, we must stumble onto an answer by trial and error. In this case, the person found that nail-biting helped to deal with the negative mental state. The relief from the negative emotion is the reward. The brain catalogues the events that preceded the award and creates a feedback loop so you can alter the strategy next time and get to the solution much quicker, without the need for trial and error each time. So, the next time you feel in the same mental state, you immediately bite your nails.

Habits are very efficient as they provide a reliable solution to a recurring problem, so the brain doesn't have to go through the 'figuring out' process each time. The brain creates "if this, then that" scripts so when we encounter the same cue in the future, it follows a pre-programmed response. The next time you come across the same cue, the routine is triggered because your brain predicts the reward based on experience. After a certain number of cycles around the loop, we stop making a conscious choice, and the behaviour becomes automatic: cue, routine, reward, all beneath your conscious awareness.

We learn most habits as children, and by the time we become adults, we barely notice those that run our lives. By understanding the essential components of the habit loop, we can consciously engineer our habits, so they have a positive impact on our lives. You can identify the recurring action required to achieve a goal and form a new positive habit, or you can reform an existing habit that is preventing you from achieving success.

So, how we can build better habits that will lead us to the future we want? Making a good habit requires an understanding of a few basic rules of human psychology:

1. Find a simple and obvious cue for the behaviour you desire.
2. Clearly define the reward and make it satisfying.
3. Understand what craving will drive the behaviour.

The lessons that follow will focus on each of these and how they can be used to help you achieve your goals.

Lesson summary:

1. A habit is a behaviour repeated enough times to become automatic.
2. The habit loop consists of a cue, a routine, and a reward. The cue triggers the routine, which gives the reward. Craving the reward drives the cycle.

Lesson #35: Raise awareness of your daily routine

"Motivation is what gets you started. Habit is what keeps you going" Jim Rohn

The first step towards engineering your habits is raising awareness of your current habits. This is critical because most of the habits we live out, we do so without conscious awareness. It is thought that as much as 43% of our daily behaviours are habits. It is not surprising when you think about it. A typical morning routine might look something like this: wake up, turn the alarm clock off, get out of bed, clean teeth, have a shower, get dressed, walk downstairs, put the kettle on, make breakfast, eat breakfast, put on shoes, lock the house, get in the car, drive to work. Even the minute details of each action, such as how you make your tea or how you tie your shoelaces are all habits. Therefore, raising awareness of your currents daily habits an essential first step and will also be useful in later lessons when integrating new habits into your daily routine.

Start by tracking your behaviours and choices. Tracking works because it makes the unconscious, conscious. You cannot manage or improve something until you start measuring it. To track your habits, simply pay attention to what you do and record it, being as detailed as you like. It can also be helpful to do this over a week to get a bigger picture of your weekly routine. This exercise will help you understand just how much of your behaviour is habit but more importantly, what times of the week your negative habits exist and how you can integrate new positive habits into your routine.

Lesson summary:
1. As much as 43% of your daily behaviours are habit.
2. Keep a log to raise awareness of your habits.

Lesson #36: Make cues for positive habits simple and obvious

"First we make our habits, then our habits make us" Charles C. Nobel

We like to think we are in control and capable of making the decision that is in our best interest. In truth, many actions we perform in a day are shaped by the simplest and most obvious option. If there is a simple cue that is right in front of us, it will trigger a habit, and we unknowingly act it out. So, if you want to form a positive new habit, the first rule is to make the cue simple and obvious.

To do this, we need to design our environment. If you want to make a habit a bigger part of your life, then make the cue a bigger part of your environment. If you're going to start running each morning before work, do you think having your running shoes in the back of your wardrobe will help, or would leaving them next to your bed be more productive? Without the cue there to spark your habit, it's very easy to miss the morning run. The simplest and most effective cues are visual. The sight of the cue will spark your behaviour without conscious awareness. A slight change in what you see can lead to a significant change in what you do.

Remember the earlier lesson where we keep the objects of our gratification out of sight. It is so we remove the cue. For habits you want to change, you must reduce or eliminate the cues from your environment. For example, remove the tray of doughnuts from the kitchen worktop where you will easily see them. Why use your willpower trying to resist bad habits when you could just remove the cue and make life easier for yourself. Design your environment in a way that will encourage good habits and eliminate bad ones. Use your imagination, the only rule is to make the cues for good habits simple and obvious, and those for negative habits invisible.

Lesson summary:

1. Make cues for positive habits simple and obvious.
2. Make cues for negative habits invisible.

Lesson #37: Give your habits a time and space to live in the world

"Good habits, once established are just as hard to break as bad habits" Robert Puller

Cues can fall into one of five categories: time; location; emotional state; other people and immediately preceding action. The next two lessons focus specifically on three of these and how they can be used to form new habits. This lesson concentrates on time and location cues, and the next is about immediately preceding actions. Of the five categories, these are the easiest to control, so we will focus on how they can be used to integrate new habits into your life.

Most of your habits not only depend on one cue but a complex mix of cues. Every habit is context-dependent; the triggers become associated with the entire context, the mixture of the five types of cues. For example, you might watch TV for an hour each night after work. The setting for this habit would be location – living room; time – 7 pm; people – your wife; emotional state – tired and stressed from work; immediately preceding action – eating dinner. The context is the specific set of cues that triggers watching TV.

Some habits will share similar elements of cues, and when this happens, the easier ones will usually win out. For example, you want to start doing more exercise and buy a running machine which you put in your living room. When faced with all the cues in your living room associated with watching TV, which habit do you think will win out: running or watching TV? Instead, create a new context for your new habit. Go out to the woods and make this the home of your new running habit. Every habit should have a home – a time and space where the habit exists, which is unique to it. If you struggle to sleep, you've probably heard the advice that you should only go to bed when you want to sleep so your brain can make the association between getting into bed and going to sleep. If you watch TV for 3 hours in bed each night, your bed becomes the home for your TV watching habit which can lead to difficulty sleeping. Each habit needs its unique place.

Habits thrive under predictable circumstances. To use time and location cues to form a new habit, you simply plan when and where to perform the routine. This is known as an implementation intention. You are giving your habit a time and place in your timetable. Studies have shown that this is an effective strategy for sticking to goals because it removes vagueness and transforms the routine into a concrete plan of action. By giving yourself clarity on exactly when and where to act, when that moment arises, you simply follow your pre-determined plan. Write down your plan in the following format: "I will <insert routine> at <insert time> in <insert location>". The goal is to dedicate the time and location to the habit and make the cues so obvious that with enough repetition, you get the urge to do the right thing at the right time.

Lesson summary:

1. Give every habit a home, a unique time and space.
2. Use implementation intention to plan when and where you will perform the habit.

Lesson #38: Use existing habits to form new habits

"You'll never change your life until you change something you do daily. The secret of your success is found in your daily routine"
John C. Maxwell

It is a characteristic of human behaviour that we will often decide what to do next based on what we have just finished doing. In other words, the sequence of our habits becomes a habit. We can use this to introduce new habits using the process known as habit stacking. One of the best ways to build a new habit is to identify a current habit then stack the new one on top. Rather than use time and location cues as with the last lesson, you use immediately preceding actions as cues. Here you will say "After <insert current habit>, I will <insert new habit>. For example, after I drink my morning coffee, I will do five minutes of yoga. Or after I shower, I will read five pages of my book. After a certain number of repetitions, you will associate the new behaviour with the current habit. The desired new habit must have the same frequency as the existing habit. For example, if you want to perform the new habit daily but stack it with a habit you do once a week, this clearly won't work. Determine the frequency of the desired habit and review those you identified in lesson 35 for established habits to use in your stacking.

Lesson summary:

1. Use habit stacking to build a new habit into your life by stacking it on top of an existing habit.

Lesson #39: Associate the cue with a craving for the reward

"A person who controls his habits can control his future" Pradip Langhe

When we receive a reward after behaving a certain way, the brain releases dopamine, which makes us feel good. When we experience pleasure, our brains work back through the previous actions to look for the cues that led to the pleasurable experience. The hit of dopamine becomes associated with the cue so the next time you come across it, you have a craving for the reward. Habits are, therefore, dopamine-driven feedback loops. A craving for the reward drives the habit loop. The next key consideration for your new habit is that the cue must trigger the craving for the reward to come. One of the first studies to explore this was performed by Pavlov and his dogs. He would ring a bell just before feeding them, and at the sight and smell of the food, the dogs would begin to salivate. This was repeated until the dogs associated the ringing bell with their food to the point where simply ringing the bell would cause the dogs to start salivating. You need to do something similar to condition yourself associating specific cues with rewards if you want to make habits stick.

The critical thing to remember is that the reward must be something we want, something that we will crave when we come across the cue, and that releases dopamine in the brain when received. It is perhaps the single biggest reason why it is so easy to have 'bad' habits. Things like gambling, drugs, and unhealthy foods all trigger release of dopamine and so it is easy for these habits to form. The rewards are obvious and immediate. Contrast this to more positive habits like reading a book, working out, or saving money, where the rewards are less obvious and immediate and don't necessarily involve dopamine. You can understand why positive habits are more difficult to form. So, what can we do to combat our biology? Below are three practical techniques you can use to make your new habits attractive and rewarding.

1. Look for any kind of reward

It can be challenging to look at your running shoes and crave a run, but it is possible. I have a pair of shoes just for running. They are bright red trail shoes, so the design is very different from my other shoes. The cue is something simple and obvious. Next is the tricky part of associating the shoes with the rewards of running.

The rewards might not seem obvious, especially if you're someone who hates running. If you've ever experienced 'runner's high', you'll know how rewarding this can feel. Traditionally, it was thought that 'runner's high' was to do with the release of endorphins in the brain after exercise; however, more recent research suggests that chemicals known as endocannabinoids are involved. These are chemicals that are very similar to the cannabinoids found in marijuana. When you feel this natural high from running, make a conscious effort to look at the shoes (or whatever else you choose as the cue), think about how they feel on your feet, smell them, whatever you need to do to make an association between them and the reward.

After enough repetition, just the sight of your shoes, the feel of them on your feet, or the smell of them will be enough to trigger a craving for the reward. Your brain will start to make the association between the cue and reward so that when you see the cue, the craving for the reward begins to develop.

2. Focus on the joy that the long-term rewards will bring you

Focus on the long-term rewards of the positive habit rather than the immediate reward from the routine itself. For example, instead of saying "I need to go for a run" say "It's time to build endurance and speed" or instead of saying "I need to save £200 per month" say "Living below my current means increases my future means". Focus your mind and your words on the long-term reward you will gain from the habit to help balance your goal-motive conflict.

3. If these techniques don't work for you, the next lesson describes a method that you may find easier.

Lesson summary:

1. Habits only form when the reward is strong enough to trigger a craving.
2. For new habits, think about the rewards and start conditioning your brain to associate them with your cues.
3. Focus on the long-term benefits of the habits rather than the routine itself.

Lesson #40: Use short-term rewards to sustain long-term habits

"Don't give up what you most want for what you want now"
Richard Scott

A craving must exist for the habit loop to form; therefore, we are far more likely to repeat a behaviour when we find the reward satisfying. Sensory impulses that trigger pleasure centres in the brain tell us "this is good do it again next time". Pleasure teaches your brain that a behaviour is worth remembering and repeating. A fundamental principle of behaviour change is what is rewarded is repeated; what is punished is avoided. Positive emotions cultivate habits; negative emotions destroy them. One of the most common reasons for people giving up on their goals is the negative feelings they associate with their routines. In other words, their brains just aren't releasing enough dopamine for them to crave the reward.

We live in a delayed return environment where work is required upfront to achieve results. The human brain evolved in an immediate return environment. When we hunted, we were rewarded with food. Because of this, we value the present more than the future, and what is immediately rewarded is repeated. The positive habits you want to form may not lead to immediate reward, and so it is difficult to develop the habit. But it's possible to train yourself to delay gratification by working with human nature and adding immediate pleasure to the habit using a technique known as temptation levelling.

In temptation levelling, you recondition your brain to enjoy an unattractive habit by linking the routine to something you find rewarding. Give yourself a small reward each time you complete the routine, and you make hard habits more attractive by learning to associate them with a positive experience. So, where the routine itself doesn't provide a sufficient reward, you manufacture something you find rewarding, which will trigger the dopamine release. For example, if you dislike running and 'runner's high' is an insufficient reward for you to crave running, insert something you do find rewarding. Allow yourself to have a small piece of chocolate whenever you complete a run. This offers you a reward that you'll find satisfying, so it increases the odds you will repeat a behaviour and sustain it long enough for the habit to develop.

The reward can be anything you like and find pleasurable but make sure it doesn't undo all the work of actually doing the routine. So, don't eat an entire box of chocolates every time you go for a run. The reward must give immediate satisfaction to fulfil our urge for instant gratification, so deliver it at the end of the routine where it will be most memorable. Where possible, keep the reward unique to the habit because if you give yourself the same reward without performing the habit, you won't associate the reward with the routine. As the habits begin to form, you'll need less outside encouragement to follow through until the point where you no longer need the short-term reward because the longer-term rewards have taken over.

Lesson summary:

1. Many positive habits don't release enough dopamine for them to be rewarding so you must manufacture the reward instead.
2. Use temptation levelling to insert a reward which you will find rewarding leading to a hit of dopamine.
3. The release of dopamine will become associated with the unattractive habit meaning you'll be more likely to repeat the behaviour.

The techniques described so far in this habit section allow you to create a simple set of rules that will guide your future behaviour. To summarise the key points:

1. Select the right cue; it must be something simple and obvious.
2. Give each habit a specific and unique cue including a time and place.
3. Use habit stacking to leverage your existing habits.
4. Train your brain to associate the cue with the reward into order to develop a craving.
5. Use temptation levelling to attach a short-term reward to the routine.

Lesson #41: Make a habit easy

"Successful people are simply those with successful habits" Brain Tracy

During habit formation, physical changes occur in the brain. The key to mastering a new habit is performing the routine a sufficient number of times for the change to occur. It is not clear exactly how many repetitions it takes to make a behaviour automatic. What is clear, however, is that what's important is repetition, rather than perfection. Don't worry too much about doing something correctly, focus on getting it done and doing it as many times as you can.

But how can you stay motivated in the short term while the habit forms? The answer is to make the habit easy. We are inherently lazy and will tend to follow the route of least resistance. This is because energy is precious, and the brain is wired to conserve it wherever possible. As such, we do what is easy. So, if you're trying to start running, only run 1 or 2 miles until the habit of running has formed. After that, run longer distances. If you start running 10 miles straight away, it will be harder to sustain the routine until the habit forms.

Work your new habits so they fit into the flow of your life. Look for and eliminate every point of friction that costs unnecessary time or energy. For example, use the gym that is closest to your home instead of the one in the next town. Remove anything that could be an excuse for you not to it your new habit.

Use the 2-minute rule to make sure you start the routine. The 2-minute rule is to make the first 2 minutes for your habit really easy. So easy that you cannot fail to do it. It could be putting on your running shoes, for example. Or getting in your car to go the gym. The gateway habit requires minimal effort, but it leads you into the habit which requires more effort.

Lesson summary:

1. Make the routine easy until you have repeated it enough times to form the habit.
2. Use the 2-minute rule – make the first 2 minutes of the routine so easy that you experience no resistance.

Lesson #42: To change an old habit, keep the cue and reward the same but change the routine

"A habit cannot be tossed out the window; it must be coaxed down the stairs one step at a time" Mark Twain

So far, we've focused on the formation of a new habit that will have a positive impact on your life. But what if you've already got a bad habit affecting you in a negative way that you want to stop? Unless you take deliberate steps to fight it, the behaviour will continue to unfold automatically. Unfortunately, habits are so powerful that your brain will never forget one, it will remain there waiting for old cues. Instead, your focus should be on changing the habit. The secret to changing a habit is to keep the same cue and reward but change the routine. When you think about it, it's the routine that you want to change. In this lesson, we will go through the steps involved in changing a habit, using smoking as an example.

1. Your current habit loop

The first part of changing your habit is to recognise each part of the habit loop.

i.   Your current routine

It is the easiest part to identify. It is the behaviour you want to change. In this example, this is smoking.

ii. The cue

Becoming aware of your triggers is the first step in habit reversal training. Most of your habits have been present for years, so you aren't conscious of what triggers them. You take in so much information at any one point that it can be challenging to identify precisely what the cue is amongst the noise of everyday life. A simple but useful method is to log details of potential cues every time you feel the urge to perform the habit. As cues fall into five categories, ask yourself the following five questions:

Where am I?

What time/day is it?

What is my emotional state?

Who am I with?

What was I doing before I got the urge?

Do this for a week or two, and you start to build up a picture of what triggers your habit.

iii.   The reward

The reward is the thing that satisfies your craving. In this example, the reward is the hit of nicotine. For some habits, the rewards are less obvious, so experiment with them to find out exactly what it is you are craving. For example, if you crave a cup of tea and biscuit during your mid-morning work break, is this because you are hungry, or you want to socialise with your colleagues? Experiment by having the tea and biscuit at your desk. If this satisfies the craving, then the food is the reward. If not, the reward is socialising with your colleagues, and you can replace the tea and biscuit with water and an apple because it is the socialising that you really crave.

2. Your new habit loop

The cues and rewards remain the same as identified in step 1.

Your new routine

This is the part you need to change, so you'll have to come up with a competing response. Whenever you encounter the cue, immediately perform another action that will prevent you from doing the old one. There are two rules for the replacement routine:

1. It must offer the same reward as the old habit; otherwise, you have no incentive to change. Your aim is to find an alternative, less destructive routine which still satisfies the craving.
2. The closer the replacement routine is to the old routine, the better. You will be more likely to adopt the new routine if it is like the old one.

Replace cigarettes with e-cigarettes. This will deliver the same reward (the nicotine), and the new routine is very similar to the old routine.

Lesson summary:

1. You cannot forget cues for habits, so instead, you must keep the cue and the reward the same but change the routine.
2. Become aware of your current habit loop and insert a competing routine which offers the same reward.

Lesson #43: Attach your identity to your new behaviour

"What you get by achieving your goals is not as important as what you become by achieving your goals" Henry David Thoreau

Often when we want to make a change, we look to change the wrong thing. There are three things we can improve:

1. Yourself – thoughts, beliefs, attitudes, and actions (the who)
2. Outcomes – the end goal or result (the what)
3. Process – the routine or system (the how)

When seeking change, many will start with the what or the how. These are usually the most obvious things. But the place to start is with yourself. Get yourself right, and this will have the greatest impact on your life.

This lesson concludes the first section of the book, where we have looked at the essential factor for your success: you. We started with your thoughts and beliefs and looked at how to change self-limiting beliefs into empowering beliefs. In the attitude chapter, we discussed some important lessons on how your attitude influences your outlook on life. Finally, we explored your actions and how to use discipline and habit in behaviour change. You have complete control over each of these. Engineer them so they work for you rather than against you, unlocking a powerful force that will transform your life.

The ultimate form of behaviour change is a change to your identity. Instead of saying "I'm the type of person who wants this" you say "I'm the type of person who is this". For example, when you say "I want to quit smoking" you're not attaching the change to your identity. Instead, say "I'm a non-smoker". State the change you want in your life, then make that change a part of who you are. Take pride in that aspect of your identity because when your ego gets involved, you'll fight to maintain the change. Improvements are only temporary until they become part of who you are.

We all go through many microevolutions during our lives, changing bit by bit, day by day. Your identity is not set in stone. You have a choice in every moment. Choose who you want to be today and reinforce that with the thoughts, beliefs, attitudes, and habits you choose. Your future self depends on it. Every thought, belief, attitude, or action you take today is a vote for the type of person you will become tomorrow. No single action will change you, but the votes build up over time. First, decide the kind of person you want to be, then prove it to yourself with small wins. When your behaviour and identity are fully aligned, you are no longer pursuing behaviour change. You're already acting like the type of person you believe and need yourself to be.

PART 2
WHAT DO I WANT?

Lesson #44: You can't hit a target you can't see

"The world has a habit of making room for the man or woman whose words and actions show that they know where they're going" Napoleon Hill

In the introduction, I said that whoever you are, you are in pursuit of something. The ultimate end goal where you experience the best from life. I have called this success, but exactly what this means is unique to you. You may have a clear picture in mind about what it means to you. If not, this section aims to help you figure it out. We will set out to answer two fundamental questions:

1. "What do I want?"

Society teaches us to behave a certain way. To comply with the norm, most of us suppress our true desires. After repeating this year after year, we can forget what we want. So, when asked the question "What do you want?", you can't respond. When you don't know what you want, how can you ever hope to achieve it? You have very little chance of hitting a target you can't see. It's all too easy to fall into this trap and never live the life you truly want.

You can achieve any goal you set for yourself. Your greatest responsibility is to invest whatever time and effort are required to become clear about what you want and go after it. We will explore the process in this section. You might already know what you want but do you have goals to make it happen, and are they written most effectively? Most who think they have goals, actually have hopes and wishes. Because they believe they already have goals, they never engage in the hard act of goal setting. Goal setting is a key skill, and we will explore how to do it the right way in chapter 5.

2. "Why do I want it?"

Knowing what you want isn't everything. You need to be clear on why you want it too. Most people will work towards something they think they want, only to realise when they get it that it wasn't what they wanted after all. By taking the time to understand why you want the things you do, you can be sure that everything you're working towards is worthwhile and meaningful. The worst use of time is working very well on something that doesn't need doing. If your ladder is leaning against the wrong wall, every step takes you closer to the wrong place. By the end of this section, you will know what you want and why you want it so you can be sure that your ladder is leaning against the right wall before you started climbing.

In chapter 4, we will start by exploring your core values and your vision. When you are clear on these, you can set the direction of your life. We will use these to brainstorm your wants and desires. When you have some ideas, we can then think about why you want these things. Only those things you have a good reason for wanting and that will contribute to your life in a meaningful way will be kept and used to generate your purpose and goals. We will explore how to set effective goals in chapter 5.

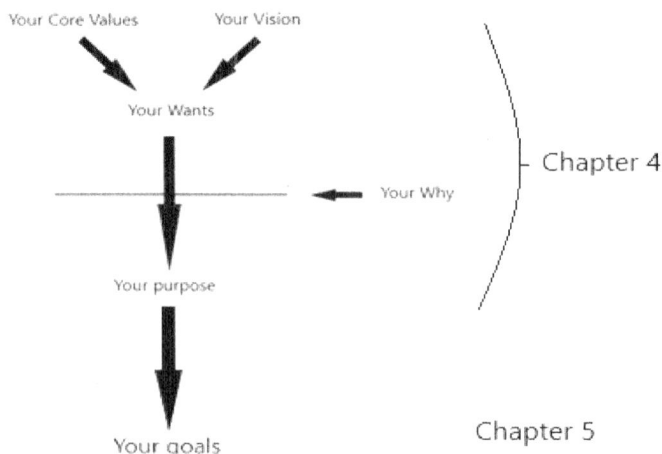

Lesson summary:

1. Become clear on what you want and why you want it so you can start structuring your life in a way that will lead you to success.

4 WHAT AM I WORKING TOWARDS?

"Whatever the mind can conceive and believe, it can achieve"
Napoleon Hill

We all have an idea of what our ideal life looks like. The image you hold is specific to you. You might have a clear picture in your mind's eye. Or the picture might be fuzzy and changes a lot. Whatever it looks like to you, you should aim to get it out of your head and onto paper because this simple act is the first step in making it real.

There are two key tools that you can use to help you become clear on what you want. These are your core values and vision. Your values are the things that are most important to you and the way you live your life. They represent your truest nature, highlight what you stand for, and guide your behaviour. They act as a personal code of conduct.

Your vision is the destination, the thing you are working towards, and want most. When your vision is clear, you have a defined endpoint that you can intentionally work towards every day. All things are created twice, first in the mind then in the physical world. Everything manmade that you see around you right now started as a thought or vision in someone's mind. You have the power to create whatever you desire, but it starts with first visualising the life you want.

In this chapter, we will take some time to think about your core values and vision which you can then use to brainstorm your wants and desires. We will then think about why you want those things and use this to 'filter' your wants. What remains should become your primary focus. By the end of the chapter, you will know what you want, why you want it, and what your purpose in life is.

Lesson #45: Live true to your values

"True success is living by your values" Dr Russ Harris

One of the most common regrets of the dying is not living a life true to yourself. To live true to yourself, your decisions and actions must be in line with your values. Therefore, if we are to live true to ourselves, we must first take the time to get clear on our values. Only then can you be confident that your decisions and actions are effective and moving you in the direction you want to go. You can ignore external pressures, which may encourage you to betray your core values and instead base decisions on what's important to you.

In this lesson, we will go through the steps to uncover your core values. You can find a list of core values online to help with this process. However, the danger of using a list is that the conscious mind will test which values appear 'better' than others. Also, you may end up choosing values you think you should have rather than being completely honest. So, before looking at examples, go through the steps below. If you struggle to think of values, use the internet for inspiration.

Step 1 – Think back

Use emotion to guide you. Whenever you've felt positive emotions, your actions and experiences aligned with your values; whenever you've felt negative emotions, you've acted against or compromised them:

a. Think back to a time in your life when you felt happy or proud of something. Think about what you were doing and why it made you feel good.

b. Now think of a time when you were angry, frustrated, or upset. Why were you feeling that way, what value might you have been compromising? Have you ever been pressured into doing something that made you feel uneasy? Why did it make you feel this way?

c. Values can also be personified in people you love or respect, so it can help to think about your role models and the values they embody.

d. What would you like people to say about you at your funeral? About your character? Your contributions? The difference you made to them.

If you're using example values, write down all those that resonant with you. Don't worry if you write a lot at this stage. It can help to understand the meaning of the words so look up the definitions of any you're unsure about.

Step 2 – Write them down

Brain dump everything that comes to mind from step 1. Make it as detailed as possible and pick out keywords or phrases that are important to you. Re-write these on a new piece of paper. Aim to write anything between 10-50 things.

Step 3 – Narrow them down

There's a good chance that you can group some values into common themes. For example, personal development is important to me, so I could select development, education, growth, and learning. I can group these because they share a common theme. Next, choose one of the values that best describes that group and use that to label the group. There is no right or wrong way to do this, just whatever works best for you. If you have a list of 30-50 values from steps 1 and 2, aim to narrow your list down to a maximum of 10 groups.

Step 4 – Rewrite your values as actionable statements

Values are often written as nouns such as integrity, bravery, honesty. The problem with nouns is they're not actionable. They're things. And it can be difficult to understand how you should behave. Therefore, for core values to be most effective, they should be converted into verbs (i.e. an action or "doing word"). Verbs give you a clear idea of how to act in any situation. Saying you have integrity doesn't guarantee it but saying you'll always do the right thing makes it possible because it becomes an explicit instruction.

Some of the suggested words are easy to convert into verbs; for example, development becomes develop, growth becomes grow, and learning becomes learn. For those that are less obvious, think about what the value represents to you and how you would instruct someone to act. Using your groups from step 3, aim to write a short, actionable statement for each. The complete statements should be concise but instructive. It doesn't matter if you can't fit all the values from a group into a sentence. Using the same example as before, my values of development, education, growth, and learning would become:

Education: grow as a person through continuous development and daily learning.

This sentence provides clear instructions, and by reading this at the start of every day, my subconscious mind will be on the lookout for opportunities of growth and learning.

Step 5 – Review your values

You should now have a list of about ten value statements that provide instructions on how to live to experience the best from life. When reviewing your list, you should be able to see a clear picture of yourself. Do your values make you feel good about yourself? Are you proud of them? Would you be comfortable sharing them with people you respect? If there are any that you aren't sure about, go back to step 1 and give them further thought.

Step 6 – Keep your value statements somewhere visible and refer to them daily.

You should now understand what matters most to you, have a sense of inner direction, and approach decisions with confidence and clarity. You can be sure that your actions do not violate the criteria you have defined as being most important and that each day of your life contributes in a meaningful way to your ultimate success.

Lesson summary:

1. To live true to yourself, get clear on your values and make decisions and actions that are in line them.

Lesson #46: Know your destination before setting off

"Cherish your visions and your dreams as they are the children of your soul, the blueprints of your ultimate achievements"
Napoleon Hill

Are you pleased with your world right now? If not, do you know what you'd like to change about it? It is thought that 98 out of 100 people who are dissatisfied with their lives do not have a clear picture in their mind of the world they would like. Can you state right now what you want? If you don't know where you're going, how can you ever expect to get there?

Defining your vision is one of the most important things you'll ever do. By knowing where you want to go, you can set off in the right direction and focus your efforts on the necessary things to reach the end destination. You can intentionally work towards it, choosing to do only those things that will bring you closer to it. In this lesson, we will explore how to get the vision out of your head and onto paper.

In his book *The 7 Habits of Highly Effective People*, Stephen Covey explains the principle of beginning with the end in mind. It means having a clear vision of the future and the desired outcome you expect to achieve. If you don't have a clear endpoint in mind, you won't know where to start, how to work towards it, or when you've reached it. Your greatest responsibility is to invest whatever time is required to become clear on what it is you want.

Sadly, most don't take the time to think about the ultimate result of their long-term goals and so go through life reacting to external circumstances rather than working proactively towards their vision. Constant distractions surround us, and it's easy to lose sight of what's important in the noise of daily life. Having a clear vision of where you want to go inspires you to focus on what matters and ignore everything else.

When you have a clearly defined vision of your ideal life, it will feel like you've suddenly opened your eyes for the first time. After stumbling through life, all of sudden you can see where you're going. You will start to see everything differently. Things either move you closer to your vision, or they don't. You'll no longer have time for the things that don't move you forward. Your daily actions become deliberate and intentional as they lead you on a straight path directly to where you want to go instead of simply drifting along and being influenced by the world around you. At the start of each day, your first thought can be "*what can I do today that will bring me closer to my vision?"*.

Craft your vision

There is no one right way to write out your vision. Create a mental image of life as you would choose to live it if you had no constraints. Aim to get as much out of your head and onto paper as you can. Use anything that captures your vision, including words and photos. Print off inspirational quotes that inspire you, anything that you find motivating. Make it as detailed as possible, so when you reach the destination, you'll know you've made it. Ask yourself questions based on the following:

1. What do you see yourself doing?
2. Where do you see yourself spending time?
3. Who do you see yourself with?

Think about what your ideal life would be like in each of the following areas:

1. Professional/Work/Career/Business
2. Financial/Money
3. Education/Personal Development/Growth
4. Intimate relationship/Love/Romance
5. Family
6. Friends
7. Health/Fitness/Wellbeing/Nutrition
8. Enjoyment/Hobby/Fun/Adventure/Recreation
9. Charitable/Contribution/Community
10. Spirituality/Emotion/Mindset

Include anything that invokes an emotional response and inspires you to make that vision a reality. Put it somewhere prominent where you will see it daily to act as a constant reminder of the life you want to live.

Lesson summary:

1. With a clear vision of your ideal life, you can do things that will bring you closer to it and avoid situations that distract you.

Lesson #47: Use your core values and vision to brainstorm what you want

"The first secret of getting what you want is knowing what you want" Arthur D. Hlavaty

You can now use your core values and vision to determine your 'list of wants'. Below is a simple technique for using your core values to stimulate ideas. We will also ask lots of questions to help brainstorm ideas. By the end of this lesson, you should have plenty written down that will act as your raw desires. We can then use these to create your goals.

1. Core values

Write out a table with three columns and the column headers, 'Value', 'Score', and 'Action Step'. Add your list of values to the 'Value' column. Go through each one separately and think about how well you are living by that value right now. Give each one a score out of ten. A score of ten means you live by this value every day, and you never abandon it despite external pressures. A score of one means that external forces easily lead you. If your score is low, you're saying that something is important to you, yet your actions don't agree. When you don't act in a way that agrees with what you consider important, you will experience negative emotions. So, for any values you score low on, think about what you can do to act more in alignment with it. For example, if you value adventure but have not been able to travel for the last few years, set yourself a travel goal. Setting goals that align with your core values is important to achieve maximum fulfilment. It ensures you have the motivation to continue through difficult times. At this stage, don't worry too much about the specific goal as we will explore how to set effective goals in the next chapter. Just note down some ideas of the things that you may want.

2. Vision

Using the ten areas of your life introduced in the vision lesson, I have created a list of questions to help uncover what you want. Try to answer them quickly and truthfully and aim to get as much onto paper as possible. The purpose of this exercise is to stimulate ideas of what you want.

1. General
   What do I want more of?
   What do I crave?
   What do I do, even though I don't want to?
   What place/person/thing brings me alive?
   What weighs me down?
   When I'm in doubt, what do I do?
   What am I passionate about?
   What are my greatest accomplishments?
   Who do I admire most?
   Who am I jealous of?
   How much free time do I want?
   Who do I want to spend more time with?

Who do I want to spend less time with?

Want do I not want?

What experiences would I like more of?

What is important to me?

What struggles or sacrifices am I willing to tolerate?

What unpleasant experiences can I handle?

If I had one year to live, what would I do differently?

What have I always wanted to do but never got round to?

2. Professional/work/career/business

What is my dream job?

What is my ideal salary?

What additional responsibilities can I take on at work?

What work do I do that doesn't feel like work?

If I started a business, what would it be?

Who do I want to serve?

What are my biggest work accomplishments and how did they make me feel?

When I look back on my career, what do I want to have achieved?

What work brings me the most fulfilment?

How long do I want to work?

3. Financial/money/investment

What do I spend money on?

What material items enhance the quality of my life?

What do I spend my money on that doesn't enhance the quality of my life?

If money were unlimited, what would I do differently?

How much money do I need each year to live my ideal life?

What is my financial freedom number?

How much money would I like in my bank account to feel secure?

What percentage of my income do I want to save and invest?

What do I want the asset allocation of my investment portfolio to be?

4. Education/personal development/growth
    What can I do to develop my skills?
    What skills do I want to develop?
    What can I do to grow as a person?
    What books can I read to develop my knowledge?
    What training courses can I attend?
    If nothing was impossible, what would I do?

5. Intimate relationship/love/romance
    What qualities do I look for in a partner?
    What compromises am I willing to make?
    What am I not willing to compromise on?
    What kind of husband/wife/partner do I want to be?
    How do I want to feel in my relationship?
    How do I want my partner to remember me when I'm gone?

6. Family

    What kind of mother/father/son/daughter/brother/sister etc do I want to be?

    Do I want to start my own family? If so, how many children do I want?

    How do I want my family to think of me?

    What role do I want to play in my family?

    How do I want my family to remember me when I'm gone?

7. Friends

    What qualities do I admire about my friends?

    What kind of friend do I want to be?

    How do I want my friends to think of me?

    How do I want to feel around my friends?

    How do I want my friends to remember me when I'm gone?

8. Health/fitness/nutrition

    What do I want to see when I look in the mirror?

    How do I want to feel in my ideal body?

    What can I do to take better care of my body?

    How do I want to feel after eating?

    What foods do I enjoy eating?

    What sports and fitness activities do I want to do more often?

    (If I have a debilitating health condition), what would I do differently if I didn't have it?

9. Enjoyment/hobbies/fun/adventure
   How do I experience joy?
   What do I do for fun?
   How do I relax?
   How do I experience adventure?
   What do I love doing?

10. Charitable/contribution/community
    What do I contribute to my community?
    How could I contribute more to my community?
    What charities would I like to support?
    What would I be prepared to do for others?
    What volunteer opportunities would I be interest in?

11. Spiritual/emotional/mindset
    How do I know when I'm happy?
    How do I know when I experience negative emotions?
    What do I think about most of the time?
    What do I do today would have made my 10-year old self cry?
    What do I need to experience fulfilment?
    How do I want to feel?
    What can I do to make me feel this way more often?

If you can answer just some of these questions, you will have a long list of things you want for each area of your life. These are your raw desires. We will now begin the process of creating your goals by applying several 'filters' to them.

Lesson summary:

1. Use your core values and vision to generate your raw desires which form the building blocks of your goals.

Lesson #48: Find a powerful enough reason why and you can do extraordinary things

"When you know your why, you'll know your way" Michael Hyatt

It's not just what you want that matters. You must also clearly know *why* you want those things. Only then will your actions be the best they can be. Whatever you're doing in life, you should always have a clear and compelling sense of why you're doing it. This applies to every action in every area of your life. When you start with thinking about why, you can set the right goals for the right reasons. If you're not clear on why, it should be your job to work out what that reason is. If there is no good reason, then you shouldn't be doing it. In this lesson, we will focus on why you wrote the answers you did in the last lesson. If there is a clear reason why you want those things, they will be kept and taken forward into the next lesson. If not, discard them.

It is not enough to have a good reason why; you must have a compelling reason. Extraordinary acts are performed when the right motivation is present. A mother can lift a car when her child is trapped underneath, or singlehandedly wrestle a polar bear to protect her child. These are the kind of powerful motivators you must look for to fight for your dreams. If you can find a powerful reason why, you'll have what you need, no matter what happens along the way. You won't take no for an answer. It's the one thing that will get you up early and keep you up late. It will light a fire in you. Anything less, and it won't be a strong enough reason to keep you motivated in the long run.

So, where can we find these powerful motivators? There are two main types: intrinsic and extrinsic. Intrinsic motivators provide an internal reward that is satisfying to you. For example, the happiness or satisfaction the goal brings you, the sense of accomplishment you feel, or the security or safety it brings you and your family. Extrinsic motivations are those things that are outside of us, such as money, praise, awards, recognition, and other benefits. Without knowing it, most people are motivated by extrinsic motivators, and these are not the compelling reasons we want. Instead, we must find the intrinsic motivators — the trick to having a powerful why is to get clear on the underlying feelings that drive you. When you do this, you will have the most reliable form of motivation available to you. Nothing will stop you.

Determine your why

To reveal your intrinsic motivators involves a technique known as the 5-whys. As the name suggests, it consists of asking why five times. Get a piece of paper and at the top, write down the thing you want. Then write down and ask yourself "Why do I want this?". Under that, write "So that…" and list all the reasons you can think. For each of the answers, ask why again. Repeat five times (or more if necessary), and you will eventually reach your powerful intrinsic motivator. If you can't find a powerful enough reason, ask yourself if you really want what you've identified. If not, discard it now. Only take forward into the next chapter the things you have an excellent reason for wanting.

With this approach, we can think about what we want in a new way, with a powerful reason why at the centre. When you do this, you can be confident that you truly want something and for the right reason. It makes us work from the inside out, opposite to how we've been trained to organise our lives. You make decisions based on what's important to you. You'll forget the things you've been mindlessly chasing, maybe out of expectation or habit, and instead focus on the things that are most important to you. When you work on and achieve the things that you have a strong reason for doing, you create a life you love living.

Lesson summary:

1. A compelling reason why you want something will keep you motivated when things get tough.
2. To determine why you want something, use the 5-whys technique.

Lesson #49: Craft a purpose statement

"The two most important days in your life are the day you are born, and the day you find out why" Mark Twain

We all want to find purpose in life. It's our reason for being here and provides us with a sense of importance. In the last few lessons, you've identified what's important to you, what you want, and why. Congratulations, you've figured out your life's purpose. If your purpose is your reason for being here, then why would you look any further than what's important to you? This is your purpose. You can be sure that when you attain the things you want, they will contribute to your life in a meaningful way. Because of this, your primary purpose from today onwards should be making it happen. Nothing is more important. Everything else is just a distraction.

<u>How to write a purpose statement</u>

A purpose statement involves putting what you want and why you want it into a statement that can act as a daily reminder of what you're working towards. Using what you've identified over this chapter, it should be easy to write a purpose statement. Simply write "*My* <insert area of your life> *purpose is to* <insert what you want> *so that* <insert why you want it>". The key thing to remember is that a purpose is not a one-off achievement. This is what makes it different from a goal. Instead, a purpose statement should give rise to an inexhaustible series of ways to push you forward. For example, the purpose statement of NASA is to "reach for new heights and reveal the unknown for the benefit of humankind". This purpose generates and drives mission after mission, each one supporting the core purpose but never completing it for good. So, aim to keep it general, and something you can always work on.

Below are some examples of my purpose statements:

1. Work purpose statement – my work purpose is to contribute to other people and make money so that I can enrich lives.
2. Growth purpose statement – my growth purpose is to continuously develop to my best self and be productive

towards meaningful goals so that I can control the trajectory of my life.

3. Financial purpose statement – my financial purpose statement is to become financially independent so that I can ensure the security and freedom of myself and my family so that we can choose how we spend our time.

4. Relationship purpose statement – the purpose of our relationship is mutual love and respect where the sum of both parts is greater than each part individually so that we can experience a lasting, loving relationship.

5. Emotional purpose statement – my emotional purpose is to live with happiness, positivity, and a focus on helping others so that I can experience the best from life.

Lesson summary:

1. Your purpose is your reason for being here.

2. Combine your 'wants' with your 'why' to generate a purpose statement, which should give rise to an inexhaustible series of new goals.

Summary

By completing the exercises in this chapter, you will know your values and vision. These are the top-level instructions from which meaningful life directing decisions can be made and can help keep you focused on the end destination. It will act as your compass, steering you through life in the direction you *actually* want to go instead of drifting aimlessly. You can begin each day with your values firmly in mind and set intentional actions that move you towards your vision. You should also have greater clarity on what you want and why you want it. You've now completed arguably the most challenging part of the process. In the next chapter, we will carry forward your desires and focus on setting goals that will drive you towards the life you would like for yourself.

5 THE GOAL SETTING PROCESS

"A goal properly set is halfway reached" Zig Ziglar

This chapter is about creating goals to help you achieve the things you want. It involves asking the series of questions shown on the next page. For your goals to be the most effective, your answers to these questions should be yes. These questions can, therefore, be thought of as the criteria for effective goal setting, and we will look at each one separately throughout this chapter. We will take the things that remain on your list from the previous chapter and ask each question to end up with your goals.

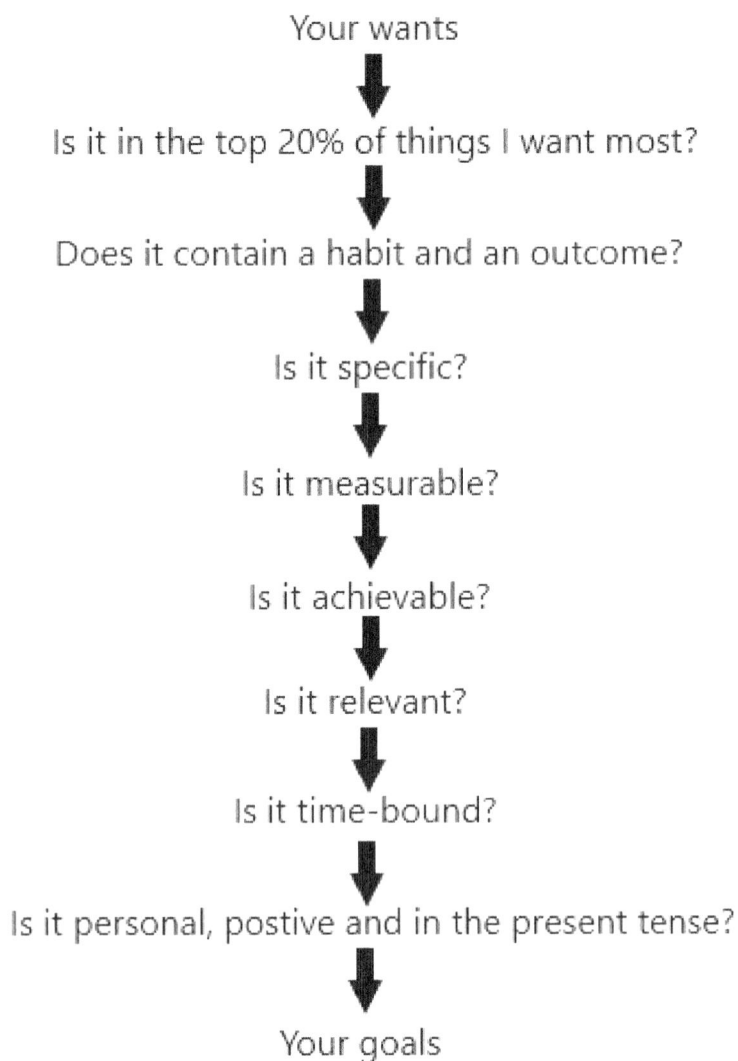

Your wants

⬇

Is it in the top 20% of things I want most?

⬇

Does it contain a habit and an outcome?

⬇

Is it specific?

⬇

Is it measurable?

⬇

Is it achievable?

⬇

Is it relevant?

⬇

Is it time-bound?

⬇

Is it personal, postive and in the present tense?

⬇

Your goals

Lesson #50: Say no to the good so that you can say yes to the great

"Every 'Yes' must be defended by a thousand 'No's'" Jeff Walker

After setting myself 100 goals for the year, some of which required significant time and effort such as running 1000 miles and learning a second language, I discovered that for effective goals, quality is far more important than quantity. It's more effective to set one goal that will move you forward in the direction you want to go than it is to set 100 meaningless goals. I thought that if I could achieve 100 goals in a year, I must be making progress in the right direction. I was doing a lot but not moving my life forward in the direction that was consistent with my vision and purpose. This lesson is about focusing on those goals that will have the greatest impact on your life and ignoring the rest.

Half-way through the year, it became clear to me that success comes from doing a small number of things very well, not lots of things half-heartedly. I had read books from some of the world's most successful people and I realised that they all shared a common trait. They excelled at one particular thing. And although they did only one thing, they did it better than anyone else, and that was enough to bring them great success. The mistake I made when setting myself 100 goals was thinking that a broad focus would lead to big success. It is the opposite: only with a narrow focus can extraordinary results be achieved.

I went through my list of 100 goals and asked whether each one was taking me closer to my vision or distracting me from it. If it took me closer, it stayed on the list, if not I removed it. In a few minutes, I had taken my list of 100 goals down to 15. For six months, I had been working towards goals that I thought I wanted. When I asked the simple question above, I realised I was wasting my time on things that weren't getting me closer to where I wanted to be. For example, I had been spending around half an hour a day learning Italian and had made some good progress; however, I realised that learning a second language didn't form any part of my vision. I could better spend the time focusing on a goal that would have a bigger impact, so I removed it from my list. Half an hour a day equates to 180 hours a year which I can now spend doing something more meaningful. In this lesson, we will remove most of what is on your list from the previous chapter and take forward only those goals that are contributing to your vision in a significant way.

Say no most of the time

Interruptions and distractions come at you from every direction. How you respond will determine the time you have available to work on the things that matter most to you. It's all too easy to say yes to things and people that distract you from what's important. But you need to practice the art of saying no. Nothing or no one has permission to distract you from your vision unless you decide to allow them. You get what you tolerate. If you tolerate things and people distracting you from what's important, that's precisely what you'll get. When you say yes to the demands of others, you effectively give them the priority and say no to yourself. But by saying no, you take back control of your time and priorities. In a world full of distractions, you must learn to focus, and this means saying no to a lot. Consider how much time the distractions cost you. For example, 1 hour of social media per day is 7 hours a week or 365 hours a year. This is more than two full weeks a year that could be better spent on you. Your success is more dependent on what you say no to rather than what you say yes to. Start being selfish, make yourself the priority, and say no.

<u>Think small using the 80/20 principle</u>

Most people think you need to go big to be successful, but it is the opposite. You must go small. Going small is ignoring all the distractions and things you *could* do and instead focusing on the few things that have the greatest impact. Not all things matter equally, and it is your job to determine those that have the highest value to you. The simplest way to do this is to ask yourself *"Is this taking me closer to my vision or distracting me from it?"*. If it moves you closer, keep it. If not, remove it.

Apply the 80/20 principle. It states that 20% of tasks lead to 80% of results. Therefore, focus only on the top 20% which will give you 80% of the results. You should aim to remove 80% of your list, leaving the remaining 20% to take forward into the next lessons. You will never get everything done. Accept this. Change 'everything' to 'the important stuff'. Get the important stuff done, and you'll succeed. If you want your achievements to add up, it starts with subtraction, not addition.

Lesson summary:

1. Success comes from doing a few things very well, extraordinary results come from a narrow focus.
2. Say no to things that distract you; your success depends on what you say no to.
3. Remove 80% of the things on your list and focus on the remaining 20%.

Lesson #51: Focus on the system as well as the goal

"Set habits, not goals because the goals which you dream to achieve will not even catch your attention after a few days, but the habits you make to achieve your goal will stay forever" Unknown

Now that you've removed 80% of your list, you should now have a small handful of things that you truly want which are meaningful to you and which will take your life in the direction you want to go. We can start to focus on the goals that will help you achieve them.

Most people set goals that depend on achieving a particular outcome, and as such, these types of goals are called outcome goals. Outcome goals are one-time achievements or milestones which are specific targets to aim for. While it is important to have sight of the outcomes you desire, setting these types of goals is not always effective. Instead, focus your goal setting efforts on the second type of goal known as process or habit goals. These are the systems or how you will reach your outcome goals. They eliminate overthinking and procrastination and require less willpower as you simply follow the system. In this lesson, we will explore the benefits of writing your goals in this way and then convert them, so they include a habit.

Benefits of habit goals

1. Control

When you set an outcome goal, your focus is on achieving that particular outcome. But we cannot always directly control outcomes. For example, you could set yourself a goal to get promoted in the next year and do everything right but still fail to meet your goal because you do not have full control over it. Outcome goals can set you up for failure. You can be the perfect employee and still not get the promotion. This will inevitably lead to negative feelings towards yourself, your company, or your boss.

By focusing your goals on your actions, which you can fully control, your success is now a direct result of your actions rather than external forces. So, change your goal from promotion, which can't be guaranteed, to something like ten sales calls each day to prospective clients. This is within your control, and if you're able to meet this goal, it could lead to your promotion. It is completely within your control whether you pick up the phone and make these calls. Remove all external factors from the goals in which you have no control and take ownership of the actions required to achieve those goals. On the next page are a few more examples to help illustrate the point.

Can you see how all the habits goals contain actions that you have complete control over? Although we cannot control the outcome, we can give ourselves the best chance of achieving those outcomes by focusing on the actions required to make them happen.

Outcome goal	Can I guarantee this will happen?	Habit goal	Can I guarantee this will happen?
Buy a house	No	Set up a direct debit to save 10% of my monthly income to go towards a deposit. Go on at least two viewings per week.	Yes
End the year in a loving relationship	No	Join a dating platform and spend 30 minutes each day contacting potential partners.	Yes
Turnover £1 million this year	No	Reach out to 20 new customers each week.	Yes
Get a six-pack	No	Spend 30 minutes each day exercising.	Yes

2. Instructive

The brain likes to receive particular instructions and setting an outcome goal that could take years to achieve doesn't provide the level of detail required in the day-to-day. Instead, provide it with information as to what to do and when to do it. For example, imagine you have the outcome goal to become a millionaire through saving and investing a percentage of your income. The outcome is important but used alone, doesn't provide instruction on how to make it happen. Instead, the habit goal of saving and investing 10% of your income into your investment account provides explicit instruction that is easy to follow.

3. Happiness

Many people pin their happiness on achieving a specific outcome goal and will only be happy if they reach it. It is a massive mistake as it means you put off your happiness. It makes no sense to restrict yourself in this way. You don't need to wait to achieve the outcome to be happy. When you focus on the habit goal, you can love the process rather than just the result. You can be happy and satisfied anytime you're performing the habit. However far away you are from the outcome you desire; you can be happy because the process is bringing you ever closer. So each month you save and invest 10% of your income you can be satisfied that the process is working and you are meeting your goals rather than saying "I will only be happy when I have become a millionaire" which could take decades. This way, you are happy today, in the knowledge that you are on the right path.

4. Sustained change

Having an outcome goal that could take years or even decades to achieve, you could find it challenging to maintain motivation and focus in the long term. Even if the outcome goal is a short-term goal, you could easily find yourself reverting to your old habits once you've achieved it and not sustain the positive change you intended. Perhaps you want to become a lifelong runner and so sign up for a marathon only to give up running after you've done your marathon. But by targeting habit goals, the actions become built-in to who you are. When a change becomes part of you, it leads to a sustained change, and the achievement of long-term outcome goals becomes inevitable.

<u>Rewrite as both outcomes and habits</u>

Both are important: without outcome goals, you have no direction; without habit goals, you have no plan. You need to articulate both types of goals. It takes some time upfront to work out the right habit goals to meet your outcome goals, but once done, you just focus on achieving your habit goals, checking in once a year to make sure your outcome goal is still relevant.

1. Determine the outcome

This is straightforward, simply write the desired outcome you want. You should have a list of 10-20 things that you want. These are probably already written as outcome goals. For example, if you want to own a house or run a marathon, they are your outcome goals. For each thing left on your list, make sure the outcome you desire is clear.

2. Determine the habit

When you break down an outcome goal, there is usually one or more actions that are repeatedly required to make it possible. To become a millionaire requires regularly saving and investing money month after month. Running a marathon requires repeatedly running day after day. Therefore, most outcome goals can be converted into habit goals.

There is a simple technique to re-write outcome goals as habits. Draw a table, with your outcome goals in the left column. In the other columns, write the following timeframes: daily, weekly, monthly, 3-monthly, 6-monthly, yearly, three years, five years, ten years, twenty years & forty years. Mark an X in the timeframe that applies to the outcome goal. Continuing with the examples above, to become a millionaire could be 20-40 years but run a marathon would be more like six months. From there, work back to the shorter timeframes and in each box, write down what you will have to do to achieve your longer-term outcome goal. Continue working back until you reach the monthly, weekly, or daily columns. At one of the shorter timeframe boxes, you will find the habit goal. To become a millionaire, work out what you would have to save and invest each month to reach the outcome goal or to run a marathon, work out how often, and for how long to run for each week or day. The exact timeframe you work back to is up to you.

3.   Write goals as habits and outcomes

Once you have identified the habit goal, you can now write out your goal, using the template below:

<Insert habit goal> so that I can achieve <insert outcome goal>.

Examples:

1.   Outcome goal: Become a millionaire
     To make this happen, I will have to save 10% of my monthly income for twenty years.
     Change the goal from 'Become a millionaire' to 'Save and invest 10% of my monthly income for twenty years so that I can become a millionaire'.
2.   Outcome goal: Run a marathon
     To make this happen, I will have to run for three hours a day, six days a week for six months.
     Change the goal from 'Run a marathon' to 'Run for three hours a day, six days a week for six months so that I can complete a marathon'.

Repeat for all the outcome goals on your list. Check that the goal complies with the benefits listed in this lesson by asking the following questions:

1.   Is this goal entirely within my control and can it be achieved by my actions alone?
2.   Is this goal instructive, and are the day-to-day actions obvious?
3.   Will meeting my daily/weekly/monthly habit goal make me happy today?

4. If I stick to this habit goal, will it lead to a sustained change in my life?

Lesson summary:

1. The benefits of habit goals include being directly within your control, instructive, contribute towards your happiness today and can be sustained in the long-term.
2. Outcome goals are still important as they set the direction; write goals so they include both outcomes and habits.

The next five lessons are based on the well-known SMART acronym, the elements that make an effective goal which stand for:

S – Specific

M – Measurable

A – Achievable

R – Relevant

T – Time-bound

We will explore each one in the next five lessons.

Lesson #52: Engage your subconscious with specificity

"Don't become a wandering generality. Be a meaningful specific"
Zig Ziglar

The subconscious mind is very powerful and to help us achieve our goals, we want this to be working with us.

Why? Because it will be on the lookout for opportunities the conscious mind might miss. Think about when you buy a new car, and suddenly, that brand and model of car is all you see on the road. You don't actually see more of that car; it is just your subconscious mind drawing your attention to it when it usually wouldn't have. Goals work in the same way. Correctly write them, and your subconscious mind will draw your attention to things that can help move you forward.

So, how can we get the subconscious mind working with us? Introduce specificity to our goals. In other words, add details. The subconscious mind needs details to spot opportunities. It spots your new car because it has the make, model and colour. Vague goals such as lose weight or earn more money are ineffective because they lack the details you need to make them happen. But when you include specific information, you will start to see opportunities all around you.

What kind of details should we include in our goals to make them specific? The aim is to be clear on the day-to-day actions required to work on the goal, as well as having a well-defined finish line. It means making the goal sufficiently detailed so that you know you're on track and when you've achieved the goal. There are no fixed rules for doing this; however, I use the following simple tricks to introduce details and instructions into my goals:

1. Add in numbers. Rather than say 'I want to lose weight', you say 'I want to lose 10 pounds'. This is discussed further in the next lesson on making goals measurable.

2. Use verbs/action words. Rather than say 'I want to lose 10 pounds' say 'Run for 30 minutes a day, five times a week so that I can lose 10 pounds'. This makes your goal a simple instruction that is clear and easy to follow, and you know when you've achieved it.

The following table provides some examples written in vague terms and then converted into specific terms:

Vague	Specific
I want more money	Transfer £200 each payday to my savings account so that I can reach my savings target of £10,000
I want to get better at my job	Spend 2 hours a day calling new prospects so that I can secure three new sales
I want a better body	Run for 30 minutes a day, five times a week so that I can lose 10 pounds
I want a better relationship with my spouse	Arrange a date night once a week so that we have at least 3 hours to ourselves.
I want to be debt-free	Set up a direct debit of £250 a month so that I can pay off my £5,000 credit card bill

Lesson summary:

1. Your subconscious mind will spot opportunities that your conscious mind might miss.
2. Engage your subconscious by introducing specific details and instructions such as numbers and verbs.

Lesson #53: What gets measured gets done

"Anything that can be measured can be improved" Michael Dell

Look at some of your goals and ask yourself the following question:

"Will I know when I'm 25%, 50%, 75%, and 100% of the way towards my goal?"

To answer yes to this question, our goals must be measurable. When we can measure our progress, it is much more likely that we will complete the goal. The simple reason for this is that as we see we are making progress, we will be motivated to continue. If you have a vague goal with no measurable, you drift along until you get bored or distracted and so it's much less likely that you'll complete it.

Measuring progress towards the goal is, therefore, an essential part of the process. It is explored in much greater detail in section 3 of the book. For now, it is enough to be aware that your goals should have built-in criteria you can measure yourself against, something quantifiable that you can track. Do a quick check on your goals and make sure they include something you can use to measure your progress. It could be money saved, weight lost, time spent, miles covered, or any other metric you can think of to monitor progress towards a target. If you used numbers in the previous lesson to make the goal specific, then the goal should already be measurable as whatever the end measure is can also be used to track progress. When you think your goals are measurable, ask yourself the question at the start of this lesson. If the answer is yes, your goal is measurable. If not, ask how I can make it measurable, so I will know when I'm 25%, 50% 75% and 100% towards my goal?

Lesson summary:

1. A goal that can be measured is more much likely to be completed.
2. Build in metrics to monitor your progress.

Lesson #54: Use short-term realistic goals as stepping stones to your dreams

"If your goals don't scare you, they aren't big enough" Ellen Johnson Sirleaf

When you think about your long-term goals and dreams, they should feel scary and overwhelming. You may feel like they are unrealistic, and you might never get there. This is completely normal. It's important to remember that the achievement of big long-term goals is simply a succession of shorter-term goals. The long-term goal might not be achievable for you right now because you lack specific skills, knowledge, or resources needed, so break it down. Your day-to-day focus should be on the realistic, achievable short-term goal.

However crazy your long-term goals might be, there is always something small that is achievable for you right now. If you want to become a billionaire but are earning minimum wage, set yourself the goal of reading as many books as you can find written by billionaires explaining how they achieved their wealth. Even for someone currently earning minimum wage, buying and reading a book is an achievable goal, and it is a step towards your long-term goal. Once you've achieved your short-term goal of reading the books of billionaires, move onto the next achievable goal, which could be to work for the company of a billionaire. If this isn't achievable, identify the skills needed to secure the job and make these the next achievable goals. There is a route from where you are now to where you want to be. You just need to work on the series of short-term realistic goals that will get you there.

If you have any unrealistic long-term outcome goals on your list, break them down into a series of smaller shorter-term realistic goals. For example, I set the goal of running 1000 miles in a year, a target that doesn't seem achievable. Instead, the shorter-term goal of running 20 miles a week is the same thing, however, seems much more feasible.

Use this simple trick wherever you have an extended timeframe for a goal by breaking down the target into a smaller timeline such as weekly or monthly. Another example is my financial freedom number. This number seems unachievable to me right now, however I know that if I can return an average of 8-10% a year on my investments and continue to invest a relatively low monthly amount, I will reach my goal. Therefore, I focus on the achievable monthly habit goal of saving a modest amount rather than what I consider the unachievable long-term goal.

It is all too common to focus on what is regarded as the unattainable end goal rather than break it down into smaller, short-term achievable goals. In believing that something is unachievable, you think it is pointless to work towards, and so you never start. Don't fall into this trap. Even seemingly unrealistic goals can be achieved in the long-term because everything you do compounds. You can achieve massive results through the compounding of small daily actions. If you can identify the shorter-term achievable goals and consistently work on them in the long term, you'll be amazed at what you can achieve.

Lesson summary:

1. The achievement of big long-term goals is simply a succession of shorter-term goals.
2. There is a route from where you are now to where you want to be; you just need to work on the series of short-term realistic goals that will get you there.

Lesson #55: Design goals for yourself, by yourself

"If you are working on something exciting that you really care about, you don't have to be pushed; the vision pulls you" Steve Jobs

Setting relevant goals is about designing goals for yourself, by yourself. If you've done the exercises up to this point in the book, you will know your ideal vision, values, your why, and purpose. You will have done the hard work already, which makes this lesson - the relevance check -

easy. Go through all the checks below to make sure you have considered them in your goal setting:

1. Would completing this goal take me closer to my vision? Think of goals as stepping stones. A relevant goal, therefore, is a steppingstone that is in the right place and moves you towards your vision, not away from it.

2. Is this goal in line with my values? Goals that conflict with your values will lead to resistance, thereby making them very difficult. Also, working towards and achieving such goals will likely leave you feeling unfulfilled.

3. Does this goal inspire and excite me into action? You're much more likely to put time and energy into something that excites you. You should have goals that make you want to leap out of bed in the morning, excited to get to work on them.

4. Am I willing to work hard to achieve this goal? If you have internal motivations to want to achieve the goal, you'll work hard to do it.

5. Does thinking about achieving this goal invoke strong positive emotions? Goals attached to your desires have a deep sense of meaning and will energise you to stay on track.

6. Is this goal in line with my why? Am I fulfilling my purpose? Chasing meaningless goals will exhaust you and is the best way to waste your life.

7. Does this goal contradict any of my other goals? You cannot be working on two conflicting goals simultaneously.

8. Is this goal relevant to my current situation? Use the steppingstone analogy again here. You can only take small steps at a time, so if you've set a steppingstone a mile up the road, you'll never reach it. The steppingstone needs to be within your reach, and this involves consideration of your current situation.

Lesson summary:

1. Relevant goals are those in line with your vision, values, purpose, and situation which inspire and excite you to stay the course.

Lesson #56: Give your dreams a deadline

"Everybody knows the power of deadlines – and we all hate them. But their effectiveness is undeniable" David Eagleman

The final element of setting an effective goal is to consider the timeframe in which it will be completed. We all have busy lives, and unless we intentionally set deadlines for our goals, they will get drowned out in the noise of daily life and not get done. Without a sense of urgency, your goals will give way to the things that shout the loudest. But by setting a deadline, you introduce a motivation to act, thereby giving priority back to your goals. Nothing motivates action like a deadline. It demands attention. The critical point is that it must be a real deadline, so if not met, there will be real negative consequences.

What is a suitable timeframe for a deadline? We can look at the effects that the wrong deadlines have on us and use this knowledge to set appropriate ones:

1. Too distant: effort dissipates to fill time, so by setting deadlines too far into the future, you risk working on goals for unnecessarily long timeframes. You have the deadline in mind and think that you have to work on the goal until that deadline comes around, rather than finishing sooner. Distant deadlines can also discourage action because you feel you have plenty of time.

2. Too tight: goals with tight timeframes can lead to stress and overwhelm, which is counterproductive. When you fail to meet these deadlines, it can also leave you feeling disappointed.

You should aim for the sweet spot in the middle, where you have sufficient time to work on the goal without being stressed but which is also tight enough to inspire action. Consider how much effort is required to complete the goal and where you can schedule this into your life. We will explore time management in more detail later.

This method can be used to determine deadlines for outcome goals; however, it doesn't work for habit goals. Instead of using a fixed date deadline, use a frequency statement and time trigger. For example, I will run for 30 minutes a day, four times a week after work.

Lesson summary:

1. Deadlines introduce motivation to act but must be real deadlines with negative consequences.
2. Deadlines that are too distant discourage action and those that are too tight cause stress and overwhelm.
3. Aim for the sweet spot in between.

Lesson #57: Check the 3Ps

"It's the repetition of affirmations that leads to belief. And once that belief becomes a deep conviction, things begin to happen"
Mohammed Ali

The final lesson in this chapter is to check whether your goals contain the 3Ps. These are:

1. Personal – every single goal you write should include 'I'.
2. Positive – express goals as positive statements rather than as a statement of avoiding or stopping something negative. Always think and talk about the things that you want rather than the things that you don't want. Your brain likes simple instructions as to what we should do, not what we shouldn't do. Telling yourself not to do something will likely make you focus on the thing you're trying to avoid. For example, don't set a goal to avoid an abusive relationship. Instead, the goal should be to find a loving relationship.
3. Present tense – write goals in the present tense as if you have already achieved them. It helps convince your subconscious mind that you can reach them.

Lesson summary:

1. Make sure goals are personal, positive, and written in the present tense.

Summary of goal setting criteria

We've gone over lots of criteria for setting a goal, and your final goals should include as many of them as you can. It is up to you to decide exactly how you want to write your goals. For me, I tend to use the following template and aim to keep it clear and concise.

<Insert why you want to achieve the goal>, I <insert your habit goal> so that I can <insert your outcome goal>.

Your why should include emotion and the use of 'I' makes it personal. The habit goal should be specific, measurable, and achievable. Include the habit frequency and write in the present tense as if you are already doing it. You should have full control over the habit. It should allow you to be happy today and lead to a sustained change in your life. The outcome goal should be specific, measurable, and time-bound however, it does not have to be realistic. The whole thing should be relevant and positive.

Examples:

1. To look and feel great, I run four times a week for at least 30 minutes so that I can maintain my bodyweight of 12 stone.
2. To secure my family's financial future and one day be financially independent, I save and invest at least 10% of my monthly income in a multi-asset mutual fund so that I can reach my financial freedom figure of £1 million by age 60.
3. To focus on all the positive aspects of my partner, I write at least one thing each day I appreciate about

them so that we can have a loving and lasting relationship for the rest of our lives.

Lesson #58: Re-write goals daily

"Write it down. Written goals have a way of transforming wishes into wants; cant's into cans, dreams into plans; and plans into reality. Don't just think it – ink it!" Michael Korda

You now have your finished goals. If you've followed the exercises in this section, you will know what you want, why you want it, and how to formulate that information into an effective goal that will maximise your chances of success. There is one last step to help increase your success rate even further, and that is to re-write your goals regularly, preferably every day.

Our brains are continually deciding what information to focus on and what to ignore. This applies to both internal information like our thoughts and external information such as what we notice in our environment. Regularly reading and writing your goals will help keep your brain primed to the things that will bring you closer to your goals and ignore things that won't. The result is that writing down goals will increase your chances of achieving them. Aim to make it a daily habit of writing down your goals first thing in the morning. Remember, you should only have 10-15 goals, so this shouldn't take you too long. If writing out your goals every day is too much, speak them out loud instead.

Lesson summary:

1. Write out your goals daily to prime your subconscious mind to be on the lookout for opportunities that bring you closer to your goal.
2. If you don't have time to write goals out each morning, speak them out loud instead.

Summary

We started this section by identifying your core values and vision, then used these to determine what you want. We then looked at why you want the things you do and the different types of motivators. When you have a compelling reason, you can be sure that you will stay the course when things get tough. Your wants and why were combined to generate your purpose statements. We then applied some goal-setting criteria to your wants which included the 80/20 principle, habit and outcome goals, the SMART acronym, and the 3Ps. The result is a list of top-quality goals written in a way that will ensure you have the best chance of success. In the next section of the book, we will explore *how* you can achieve your goals.

PART 3
HOW DO I ACHIEVE WHAT I WANT?

Lesson #59: Figure out your path to success

"An idiot with a plan will beat a genius without a plan" Warren Buffet

So far in this book, we've explored you, what you want and why you want it. When you're clear on these things, you're already way ahead of most. You know your start and endpoint, and your driving force. Knowing this is a critical first step as it sets the direction of your path. But unless you know how to lay your path, you'll be stuck at the start. The final section of this book will focus on how to achieve your vision.

If you have the *"I don't know where to start"* mentality, you must change this to *"I will find out how to get started"*. By saying you don't know where to start, you are closing the door before you even get going. You tell yourself you can't do something and so you don't take action. Instead, ask *"how can I…?"* For example, instead of saying *"I want to be a millionaire but don't know where to start"*, say *"I want to be a millionaire, how can I make that happen?"* By asking the question, you leave the door open for an answer. It stimulates creativity and makes things seem possible. Asking how forces you to think about what needs to be done to achieve a goal.

Unsuccessful people wonder whether something is possible for them, and if they decide it isn't, they never get started. I guarantee there is a route from where you are today to where you want to be. You just have to find out what it is. From this point forward, you must believe that anything is possible. You just have to figure out how to make it happen. This section is broken down into three chapters: the start, the middle, and the end of your path. The beginning includes lessons on overcoming resistance as well as time and work management systems. The middle is about keeping your momentum going and monitoring progress. The final chapter is about reaching your end destination and includes lessons on getting over the finish line, defining and celebrating success, and feeding back lessons into the goal-setting process. By the end of this section, you will have the tools you need to lay your path to success.

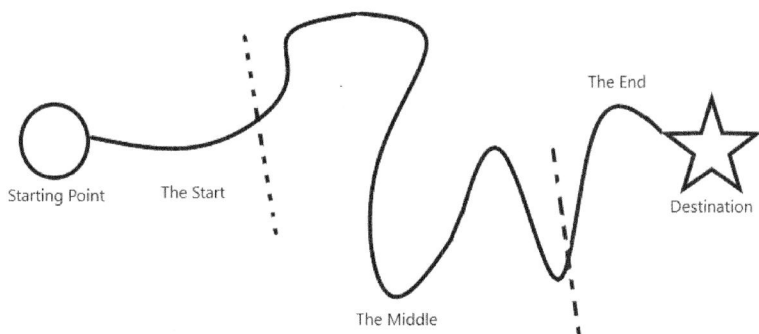

Lesson summary:

1. This section of the book focuses on how to lay the path from where you are to where you want to be.
2. Ask how to stimulate creativity and leave the door open for an answer.

6 THE START
TAKE ACTION

"Well begun is half done" Aristotle

You now know what you want, and you've written down your goals, perhaps for the first time. Now comes the hard part of taking action. But suddenly you experience some resistance and can't seem to start. We can experience resistance in many ways including waiting to be perfect before starting; giving priority to low-value activities and procrastinating; feeling too overwhelmed or fearful to start, lacking confidence, and giving in to temptations, distractions, and interruptions. Even when we're ready to act, we can still find a million reasons not to. We encounter so many possible sources of resistance that stop us from moving. This chapter aims to explore some of the main reasons why we struggle to get started, so we can overcome any resistance we feel and take action towards our goals.

We will explore the following forms of resistance:

1. Perfectionism
2. Procrastination
3. Overwhelm
4. Lack of confidence
5. Fear
6. Risk
7. Lack of time
8. Poor organisation

For each, I will put forward practical solutions to help you overcome whatever resistance you may be feeling so you can take the first steps on your path to success.

Ultimately, action is the only thing that will change your life. You can do everything else in this book, have the perfect mindset, and know what you want, but you will not get those things unless you are courageous enough to take action.

Lesson #60: If something's worth doing, then doing it is better than not doing it, perfectly

"If you are not embarrassed by the first version of your product, you've launched too late" Reid Hoffman

Most people might consider perfectionism to be a strength as you'd think it makes everything you do the best it can be. The reality is that perfectionism is a resistance mechanism and has many pitfalls that ultimately lead to inaction. In this lesson, we'll explore what perfectionism is, its downside, and how you can overcome it.

To understand what perfectionism is, we need to consider what causes this behaviour. At its root is the fear of failure. We hate to fail. We've grown up with a school system that ingrains this philosophy into us from a young age. So, to protect ourselves from failing, we use perfectionism as the defence mechanism. We want perfection before action: before starting a business, we want the perfect business plan, before getting married we want the perfect relationship, before releasing our product to the market, we want it to be perfect. We tell ourselves that if we make things perfect before starting, we can control the outcome and will never have to face failure, criticism, or disappointment again. We do everything ·we can to maintain this false sense of control, and this means we never put ourselves in a position where we fail. The result is you delay action and never get started on what's important to you.

Perfection does not exist

Facebook's Chief Operating Officer Sheryl Sandberg writes about the 'Done is better than perfect' approach in her book, which acts as a reminder to let go of impossible standards. She writes that *"Aiming for perfection causes frustration at best and paralysis at worst"*. Your focus should be on getting it 80% right. The other 20% can be modified later and released as a new version.

When a software developer works on a product, it's normal to hold off release until it's got a particular feature, or it's gone through another round of testing. It's notoriously difficult to declare a software product finished. There's always something more that could be done. The most successful developers get their product to a good enough standard, get it out, receive feedback, make modifications then release a new version. This includes companies such as Microsoft and Apple, which is why you see a new version of Windows released every few years, or a new software update on your phone.

In the same way that software developers get to a good enough standard and ship their product, you need to get to the level where you consider yourself 80% happy and take action. It is so easy to lose sight of this and get lost in the minute details and endless improvements. By releasing your 'good enough' product, you can start to build your knowledge, and along the way you learn more than you'd ever have learnt by trying to be perfect. It is also quite likely that you discover the 'perfect' product you were initially striving for was wrong anyway.

One of the biggest problems in thinking something is perfect is it doesn't leave any room for improvement. In saying something is perfect, you are effectively saying that it can't get any better and so you won't bother developing it any further. So much of what we do and who we are is limitless and thinking otherwise prevents us from growing. If I thought this book was perfect, I would make no effort to improve it. But knowing that perfection does not exist, motivates me to continue working on it even after its release. The same holds for you. You can always improve and grow. Our potential is limitless, so don't use perfection as an excuse to stop developing. We are never the finished product. Everything you release to the world is only ever a draft of the next version. Instead of aiming to release the perfect version of yourself, consider 80% to be your new level for this moment in time and strive for continuous development for the rest of your life.

Shoot your ducks

We've all heard the term, *"I'm just getting my ducks in a row"*. Well, this is perfectionist talk for *"I'm too scared to act"*. Below is some practical advice for shooting your duck so you can overcome resistance from perfectionism.

1. Acknowledge it

If you're a perfectionist, chances are you're already aware of it. But you probably think it's a strength. Acknowledge perfectionism for what it is, a defence mechanism against judgement and failure. Acknowledge that perfection does not exist.

2. Catch yourself when you go into perfectionist mode

Listen to what you say to yourself. If you hear yourself saying things like *"I just need to work a bit more on this before I start"* or *"I'm getting all my ducks in a row"* you're in perfectionist mode. As soon as you hear anything like this, imagine shooting the ducks.

3. Break the cycle

Perfectionism stems from fear. We will look at fear later and explore how we can break our patterns by replacing our responses to fear with something else. So, when you feel the fear rising in you when it's time to act, replace your old behavioural response (perfectionism) with something else.

4. See the opportunity, not the problem

If you go to your favourite bakery for a cake and see that the queue is long, how do you react? Do you see the problem of the line and give up? Or the opportunity of the reward? Focus on all the benefits that taking action will bring you. You will have the chance to gain valuable knowledge and feedback you wouldn't otherwise have.

5. Recognise when you are at the 'good enough' or 80% standard

Just because you aren't perfect, does not mean you can't still be meaningful and productive. Get to your 80% level, take action, and develop along the way.

Lesson summary:

1. Perfectionism is a defence mechanism against the fear of failure which leads to inaction
2. Perfect does not exist, so get to the 80% 'good enough' standard, get it out there, learn from the feedback and upgrade to the next version

Lesson #61: Eat that frog

"First things first, second things never" Shirley Conran

The time now comes for perhaps the two most important words in the book: take action. But before you do, you just quickly check social media, or tidy your room, or wash the car or do something equally unimportant to put off what is truly important and life changing. You start procrastinating because you've spent so long preparing yourself that when the time comes to act, it feels overwhelming. You don't know where to start, so you don't. You find any excuse to say "I'm busy with this *important* task, I'll get to that other stuff when I'm done". Then you find something else and say the same thing and become trapped in a cycle of never-ending procrastination. By the end of this lesson, you'll know exactly where to start, and by making it a habit, you'll overcome procrastination every time.

The Brian Tracy book *Eat That Frog* inspires this lesson. The book is about overcoming procrastination, and the idea is that if the first thing you do each day is to eat a frog, whatever else you have to do will be easy. And you need to eat it instantly, don't sit back and look at it for long because you'll think of all the reasons why you can't do it. Don't worry, this is only a metaphor for doing your hardest or most important work first each day.

Deciding what's important

Your ability to choose between the important and unimportant is a crucial determinant of success. But the distinction can be confusing, especially when you're trying to avoid the hard, meaningful work. And confusion inevitably leads to procrastination. You need to get clear on what is the most important task for you each day. Every action you take will have consequences. If a task is important, it will have potential long-term positive consequences and move you closer to your vision.

Starting from your long- and medium-term goals, break these down into key milestones. For you to hit these targets, what must you complete each year? To meet your yearly objectives, what must you do each quarter then each month, each week, and finally each day? By reverse-engineering your goals, you can be confident that your daily actions will have a positive impact on your weekly targets; your weekly actions will have positive consequences on your monthly targets and so on.

Coming up later in the chapter, we will explore how you can design your work so that no thought is required at the start of each day. Overthinking also contributes to procrastination, and we will remove this by pre-planning your day. We will introduce the concept of your leader brain (organisation) and worker brain (task completion). The job of your leader brain is to plan your day such that when you start work, you only use your worker brain. Your worker brain cannot procrastinate; it has been given specific instructions and must take immediate action.

Lesson summary:

1. Your most important work can be overwhelming, which leads to procrastination.
2. To overcome procrastination, start each day with the most difficult and important task.
3. To determine what your most important task is, reverse engineer your long-term goals.

Lesson #62: Knock over the first domino

"If we are facing in the right direction, all we have to do is keep walking" Ancient Chinese Proverb

We've all heard of the domino effect but what you might not be aware of is that the energy of a falling domino can knock over the next one that is one and half times bigger than itself. This means that if you lined up thirteen dominoes, the first one at just 5 mm high and 1 mm thick could knock over a domino 3 feet tall, weighing 100 pounds at the end of the chain. That equates to 2 billion times more energy between the last two dominoes than the first two. Why does this matter? While you should be looking to do your most important work first each day, it can be difficult to jump straight into it.

Newton's first law says that objects at rest tend to stay at rest and those in motion will remain in motion. What this means is that the most energy-intensive part of the process is going from a standing start to moving. So, to make the start easier, we can use the same trick as the dominoes. Make the first part of the task easy so that it requires little effort. So little effort that you can't fail to do it. This could be to turn on your computer before typing more pages of your book or to put on your running shoes before going on your morning run. The main task of writing or running could be met with resistance; however, the gateway task is straightforward, so you will find it easier to get started.

By taking the first simple step, you've gone from a standing position to moving and already overcome the most energy-intensive part. This creates momentum, a powerful force that drives you forward and sets off a chain reaction which makes subsequent tasks a lot easier. So, to help you start moving, focus on taking the first straightforward step. Once you've done that, you'll have generated momentum for the next task, then the next, until you're in flow with the main task. Your job is to line up the dominoes, starting with the smallest one first, then knock it over to generate the momentum you need to complete the big task at the end of the chain.

Lesson summary:

1. The most energy-intensive part of the process is the start, moving from a standing position.
2. Reduce the energy input required by focusing on the first simple task.
3. Like falling dominoes, this creates momentum that sets off a chain reaction, driving you forward until you can easily complete the big task.

Lesson #63: Lay your path to success one brick at a time

"The rule is simple: you go as far as you can see and then when you get there, you will always be able to see further" Zig Ziglar

If thinking about the end goal overwhelms you, all you need to do is break it down into smaller, more manageable steps. You don't have to see the end from the beginning; you just need to see the next step. In fact, you shouldn't be able to see exactly how you'll achieve it. If you can, your goal isn't big enough.

Think about the route from where you are now to where you want to be as a brick road. Instead of focusing on the entire road, concentrate just on the next single brick. The brick by brick approach makes you focus on steps (the how) rather than on the huge picture (the outcome). Focus on the next small step and when you get there, focus on the next small step after that. When you do this, it eliminates feelings of overwhelm. When I started writing this book, I felt overwhelmed by the thought. But I followed the brick by brick approach and broke it down into small steps. As I kept focusing on the next small step, the structure of the book started to evolve, and before long, I had the first draft. Your job is to go as far as you can see at this moment in time. When you get there, you will always be able to see further.

Why this approach works

Focusing on the next small step is manageable. And if something is manageable, it gives you the control. Instead of getting stuck on the image of the finished product, you simply pick up the next brick and take the small step forward. It's so much easier to see a single brick in front of you than it is to see the complete path. You may find it difficult to convince yourself that you're capable of achieving the big end goal; however, it will be easier to tell yourself that you're capable of moving forward one brick at a time. Any goal is manageable, one small action at a time.

It's also flexible. You will have to adjust your direction as you work towards your goal and because you're thinking in the form of bricks, you can be flexible. You might think you have the most direct route when you start. But as you begin to move along your path, you learn new information that will influence where you put your next brick. You'll soon find you're heading in a much different direction to the route you originally planned. Compare this to if you already had a fixed path in mind from the start. You'll be focused on doing it just one way and be less open to new information along the way.

We like to think about the big stuff, and it's great to have big dreams and a vision, but it can be dangerous if you focus only on these as it can lead to overwhelm and inaction. But by focusing on the next small step, you take control, and you'll learn things along the way that will help you make the next step. Every single brick is a valuable move forward. Every seemingly insignificant action, when stacked on top of one another, leads you to success. Pave your way to success, one brick at a time.

Lesson summary:

1. Focusing on the completed picture or end goal can be overwhelming.
2. Instead, focus on the next small step to combat overwhelm, as it puts you in control and is manageable and flexible.

Lesson #64: The formula to confidence is 3Cs

"Nothing is impossible. The word itself says I'm possible!"
Audrey Hepburn

To take action, we must be confident in our ability to perform the necessary steps. But here's the thing: when you start something that you've never done before, you're unlikely to have the confidence you need in your abilities. This is entirely normal. Unfortunately, so many of us don't understand this and give up prematurely or worse, never start. To, to help combat this, we must break down confidence into its parts and learn how to become confident. Only by doing so, can you work through all the stages required to reach the confidence level needed to act.

The steps to confidence are:

1. Courage
2. Commitment
3. Capability

Lack of confidence can have a massively detrimental effect on your life. It can stop you from pushing yourself whether this is going to the gym, asking someone out, or starting your own business. Missed opportunity and regret are often the results. Imagine the following scenario. Exactly one year ago today:

1. You started working out, and now you're in the best shape of your life. You feel incredible, and when you look in the mirror, you love what you see.
2. You asked out that person you admire. They said yes, and you've shared some amazing experiences with them over the last year and are now in love.
3. You started a side business, it's been difficult, but you've now paid off your start-up debts and out-earn your 9-5 in half the time, freeing up some time to do more of the things you love.

Think about how good you feel about your life, having had the confidence to act in all three areas. Now imagine how you'd feel if none of these things happened because you didn't have the confidence to take the first step. You're still out of shape, single, and work in a job you hate. Think about how different your life would be today if you'd had the confidence to do everything you wanted to do.

The missed opportunities due to lack of confidence can be enormous. The saddest thing is you don't even realise the full extent because the positive things you could have in your life never materialise. There is a theory called 'Many-Worlds' that states that if an action has more than one outcome, the universe splits at each point of decision. Imagine a straight-line representing your life; when you're faced with a decision, you reach a fork and there are many possible routes forward. You only ever get to travel one route and experience one possible outcome, all of the others never materialise. The route you take depends on your decision.

Imagine another version of yourself living in a parallel universe where, at every point of decision, you'd had the confidence to do what you wanted. Yes, you would have faced more rejection, but in the end, you would have a lot more of the things you want in your life. Which version of the person would you rather be? From this point forward, decide to be the one with abundant confidence. The one who went to the gym, asked out that person, and started their business. The one who is now thriving in all aspects of life. One year from now that could be you.

It's not the smartest people that become the most successful. It's the most confident. A confident person will take action to improve their circumstances. The confidence you have in yourself and your abilities is, therefore, one of the most significant factors influencing your success. Most people think about what they want to do; then how capable they are of achieving that goal. They pin their confidence level purely on their current capabilities. The problem with this approach is that to get to new levels in your life, you must go beyond your existing abilities.

However, there is a different way: learn how to be confident. Everything is learnable. Confidence is the same; you must learn how to develop it. There is no such thing as a confident person or a non-confident person; you've either learnt how to be confident with a skill or you haven't. So, if you're reading this thinking "I'm not a confident person and never will be", you just haven't learnt how to become confident yet. I've always considered myself to lack confidence. So, I decided to search for information that would help me become a more confident person. And I found a simple but effective formula: the 3Cs.

1. The <u>courage</u> to step into the unknown and face your fears
2. The <u>commitment</u> to stick with it long enough
3. The <u>capabilities</u> required to become confident

Over the next few lessons, we will look in detail at how to develop courage and overcome fear, write a commitment contract, and create a personal curriculum for developing your capabilities.

Lesson summary:

1. Confidence is the difference between acting or not.
2. Confidence is learnable if you go through the three Cs: courage, commitment, and capability.

Lesson #65: If you want something you don't currently have, you have to do something you've never done

"The fears we don't face become our limitations" Robin Sharma

Right now, do you have an area of your life you want to change or improve? If so, why haven't you already? Most likely because you're happy to remain in your comfort zone where you feel safe and in control. Your current performance is enough to meet your needs with little or no effort or stress. Life appears to be good in your comfort zone. The only problem is you want more than you're currently getting, and you won't find it by staying in your comfort zone.

Everything you have now is a result of what you have done up to this point in life. If you continue doing the same things, you'll continue to get the same results. So, what got you this far, won't get you to the next level. Only by doing something you've never done before will you get something you've never had. You, therefore, must leave your comfort zone. Over the next few lessons, we will look at what it takes to move from your comfort zone, through your fear zone and into the learning and growth zones. The figure on the next page shows the journey you will make from the comfort zone to the growth zone.

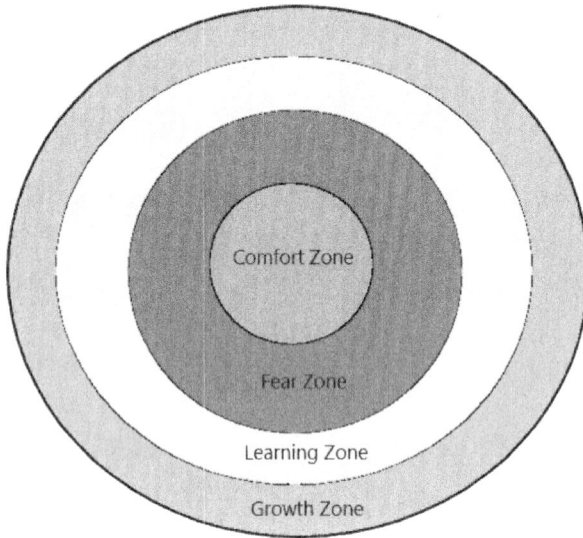

Leave your comfort zone behind

The first part of the journey is to leave your comfort zone. In case you need any encouragement that this is the right thing to do, consider the following. There is evidence that those who excel in their fields spend the most time out of their comfort zones. A study has been done that correlates the time an individual spends outside of their comfort zone with their achievements. Those who spent the most time outside their comfort zone (the top 1% of all participants), were the highest achievers in their field; this includes the top-performing athletes and entrepreneurs. This is not a coincidence; these people have become successful by always challenging themselves to extend the boundaries of their competences. Success is highly correlated to time spent out of your comfort zone.

Standing between you and growth is fear

"Everything you want is on the other side of fear" Jack Canfield

Let's assume you decide to leave the comfort zone behind because you want more. Beyond the boundaries of your comfort zone lies the second challenge: the fear zone. The fear zone is the most difficult to navigate and has likely kept you confined to your comfort zone for years. There is no way around it. You must pass through it. We will discuss techniques to help you get through it. As the quote above says, everything you want is on the other side of fear. Whenever you feel fear, use it as an indicator that you are on the right path. We tend to see fear as a warning to say stop, go back, but what it says is go this way. If something scares you, it means there's magic on the other side. Let the discomfort guide you towards significant accomplishments. If you want to achieve extraordinary things in life, you're going to spend a lot of time out of your comfort zone. So, get comfortable.

Lesson summary:

1. What got you to this level in life, won't get you to the next.
2. If you want to take your life to the next level, you must leave your comfort zone behind.
3. To get to the learning and growth zones, you have to pass through the fear zone.

Lesson #66: Courage is not the absence of fear but acting despite it

"Courage is resistance to fear, mastery of fear, not absence of fear"
Mark Twain

When we see those who appear fearless, we assume they don't feel fear. But this is not the case. Fear is an evolved response; it is part of human nature and is not something we can choose to switch on or off. It is part of who we are, and we must learn to live with it. This is where courage comes in. Courage is not fearlessness; it's facing your fears and taking action despite feeling those feeling.

<u>All new things start with courage</u>

We have a natural tendency to seek security. We want to be sure of the outcomes of the actions we take. Because of this, we stick to things we've done before as we can draw on our previous experiences to help us be more certain. When starting something new, you have no experience to draw on and so cannot be sure what the outcome will be.

The decision to cross from the comfort zone into the fear zone starts with courage. When you have no prior experience to draw on, you must rely on courage to do something for the first time. Courage is walking through a door and not knowing what is on the other side. It is taking determined action towards a life-enhancing goal despite feeling fear. Sometimes you must decide to do something without knowing what the outcome will be.

Everyone feels fear. The difference is that successful people act despite their feelings. They know that they must push through the fear zone to get to the learning and growth zones. They use fear as a sign they are on the right path and don't allow it to push them back in their comfort zone. Your ability to confront, deal with, and act despite your fears is key to your success. Learn how to master fear, and you develop the courage to act when others don't. In the next lesson, we will learn how to master fear rather than be controlled by it.

Lesson summary:

1. We all feel fear when trying new things.
2. Courage is acting despite feeling fear.

Lesson #67: Shut the FUD up

"Fear has two meanings: 'Forget Everything And Run' or 'Face Everything and Rise.' The choice is yours" Zig Ziglar

In this lesson, we will explore how to confront and deal with your fears, so they no longer prevent you from taking action towards the things that matter most to you. Fear, uncertainty, and doubt (FUD) keep too many of us paralysed and stuck in our comfort zone. But it doesn't have to be this way. We can change our old patterns, so they work for us.

The fear cycle

There are probably elements of your life right now where fear is controlling you in some way. You may hide it well or may not be unaware that fear motivates your actions. When you first encountered a fear, you learnt how to respond in a way that dealt with the unpleasant feeling. This involved distancing yourself from it, and so the uncomfortable feeling disappeared, and you returned to a calm state. When you separate yourself from the source of your fear, you stay in your comfort zone, and nothing changes for you. By learning how to silence the fear, you learn how to stay safe the next time you encounter the source of the fear. Your behavioural response to fear eventually becomes a habit and so you repeat the same patterns of behaviour over and over again. This pattern is the fear cycle and is illustrated below.

The fear cycle

Source of fear

Calm state

Feeling fear

Destructive
behavioural response

Nothing changes

Inaction

Until you notice your patterns, nothing is going to change. The secret is understanding what fear feels like to you and how it triggers you to respond. If you can change your response to fear, you can change your patterns and take control of your life. To do this, you must introduce a new behavioural response that allows you to control fear and remain in a calm state. From there, you can act despite feeling fear. This is how you develop courage, and the courage cycle is illustrated below.

The courage cycle

Source of fear

Positive change

Feeling fear

Action despite fear

New behavioural response to control fear

Calm state

Identify and change your patterns

The following 3 step process walks you through how to identify the key parts of your fear cycle including the source of the fear, your physical and behavioural responses to it, and how to break the pattern by consciously introducing a new response.

1. Identify the fear

No problem is ever fixed until it's identified. The first stage is to admit that you're afraid and identify the source of that fear. We can often struggle with this as we think fear is a sign of weakness. So instead, we act strong, hide our fears, and stay trapped as the fear dictates what we do. Ask yourself whether there is something you want to do but aren't able to get? If so, fear is keeping you trapped. The good news is identifying your fear is a straightforward process.

Fear causes a physiological feeling in your body, which we can use to pinpoint what we're afraid of. To identify your fear you must become aware of how you feel when fearful. It could be an increased heart rate, a sinking feeling in your stomach, sweaty palms, a hot flush, or any other physical reaction. Think back to the last time you felt this way. What was causing you to feel like this? This is the source of your fear. If you are struggling to think back, wait until the next time you feel it. It is important to understand the source of your fear, but the aim here isn't to avoid it. To change your life, you must confront your fears.

2. Identify your behavioural response to fear

In response to the unpleasant physical feelings you are experiencing, you will behave in a certain way to hold onto a false sense of control. Think about how you behave to silence the fear. For example, for years I wanted to start a property business, but when the time came to take the plunge and commit, my heart would race, and I would get a sinking feeling in my stomach. This physiological response triggered my behavioural response which was to find any reason not to go for it. The result was that I didn't start my business and didn't change my life. I was fooling myself into a false sense of control because my behaviour was alleviating the unpleasant feelings of fear and making me feel safe.

3. Replace your old pattern with a new pattern

Now that you are aware of how fear feels to you, the next time you start to feel this way, consciously change your response to it. Introduce new, more productive patterns. There are some simple breathing exercises you can do to relax your vagus nerve, which can turn off your fight or flight stress response. This involves breathing in for six seconds, holding it for six seconds then exhaling for six seconds. Repeat this ten times and by doing this, you can return yourself to the calm state you desire, can think clearly, and take action on the things that matter to you, despite feeling fear. By practising the breathing exercises when you feel fear, it will become your automatic response, and you will change your patterns from the first cycle shown above to the second cycle.

You now have the knowledge and self-awareness to change your responses to fear and develop courage. It's easy to revert to autopilot and go back to your old patterns because they're familiar and have kept you safe up to now. They served a purpose, but when you let them control you, you're permitting those things from your past to decide what is right for you today. You can interrupt your old patterns; you get to decide what happens and whether your fears will hold you back.

Lesson summary:

1. Fear is a habit you have developed because it kept you safe.
2. Identify and change your responses to fear if they don't serve you.

Lesson #68: Get some perspective

"If you change the way you look at things, the things you look at change" Dr Wayne Dyer

Fear can paralyse us and make us sacrifice so much. And for what? An imagined future which is most likely wrong anyway. To change the way we look at fear, we need to get some perspective. We all have days where we think the universe is out to get us. But when you take a step back and see life for what it is, you'll be much calmer. In this lesson, we will go through a technique to help you gain perspective to help you deal with your fears. It involves answering a series of questions to change the way you look at fear.

1. What's the worst that can happen?

When you ask this question, your brain will probably run wild imaging hundreds of horror stories. Play along with this and boil down the possibilities to one realistic worst-case scenario. Will you die or be physically hurt in some way? Will you go bankrupt or lose your house? Doing this allows you to figure out the worst possible outcome which we will use as our starting point. It's all up from here.

2. How likely is the worst-case?

This can be a difficult one to answer. Think about whether it's ever happened to you before or anyone else you know. Do some research to find out some statistics. For example, if you want to start a business, research how many fail in the first year.

3. Is there anything I can do now to prevent the worst-case scenario?

Of course there is. Even if your worst-case scenario is something awful and has a high chance of happening, there is always something you can do. We will look at this point in greater detail in lesson 70.

4. Can I recover if the worst-case happens?

Even if the worst-case does happen, can you recover from it? Unless it is something that permanently debilitates or kills you, you can probably recover from it. For most of the fears we have, the worst-case isn't going to be the end of your life.

There are a couple more questions to ask yourself to help shift your thinking away from all the bad things you fear to all the positive things that await you.

5. What will happen if I do nothing?

What is your fear causing you to sacrifice? Is this a price you're willing to pay to maintain your false sense of control and safety? More often than not, what you suffer when you stay trapped by fear is much worse than facing your fears.

6. What is the best-case scenario?

We are often so focused on protecting ourselves from the worst-case scenario that we miss out on so many opportunities. Things *can* go in your favour. Realise that your fear is exaggerated and keep in mind all the positive things that await you in the best-case scenario.

Once you've learnt how to conquer fear, it goes away for life. But hide from it, and it lingers. The decision is down to you. Get some perspective on your fears to help you make the right decision. The next time you have a bad day, ask yourself whether you believe that life is out to get you. That out of the 7 billion people on earth, all the planets and stars align just to get you. I don't think so.

Lesson summary:

1. To change the way we look at fear, get some perspective by asking the questions in this lesson.

Lesson #69: Your idea of safety is an illusion; embrace risks worth taking instead

"If you risk nothing, you risk everything" Geena Davis

Our fears are designed to keep us safe. But in finding safety, we often don't act in our best interests. Speak to the average person, and they will tell you that investing in the stock market is risky. Instead, they prefer to keep their money in a savings account because it is 'safe'. What the saver is doing is sitting on the sidelines because they're not prepared to risk anything. They don't realise the sideline is the most dangerous place to be because you risk losing out on so much opportunity. Their focus is on the potential loss rather than the chance to gain.

Flip a coin

We're going to flip a coin, and if it lands on tails, you lose £100. The question is, how much do you want to win if it lands on heads, for the bet to be worth the risk? I bet it's more than £100? Most will want the chance to win at least £200 for them to risk losing £100 in a 50:50 gamble. Yet the probability of winning and losing are the same, so all things being equal, we should be willing to take the bet if the gain is only £100. But we're not. The reason for this is we feel the pain of loss more than the reward of an equivalent gain. If you risk £100 to win £200, you are saying that the pain of losing £100 is the same as the joy of winning £200. Another way to put this is you feel the pain of loss twice as much as you feel the pleasure of winning. This phenomenon is known as loss aversion. Loss aversion can explain many other things, including why people stay in dead-end jobs. The fear of losing a steady paycheck is greater than the potential happiness of finding a job you love.

It might seem as though loss aversion is irrational, but evolution has made pain more urgent than pleasure, since avoiding pain is more critical for our immediate survival. So, we play it 'safe'. The safe option is saving your money in a bank account, earning no interest. Saving £250 a month for 40 years, you will have a total of £120,000. But invested in the stock market achieving an average annual return of 7% (the long-term historical average), you'd have £620,000. The safe option has cost you half a million pounds. Yet we see safety as a good thing, thinking it looks out for us and protects us from painful losses. But the opportunity cost is far higher.

To take your life to new levels, you need to reframe your idea of safety. If you decide to sit on the sidelines for security because you're not prepared to risk anything, don't fool yourself that you're playing it safe. You're risking most by doing this because you risk losing out on so much and never being able to experience the best from life. Once you understand and accept that safety is an illusion, it liberates you to embrace risks that are worth taking.

The final thing to say about risk is that it's inversely related to capability: the higher your ability, the lower the risk. I'm sure if you needed surgery, you'd be willing to let a well-trained surgeon with decades of experience operate on you, but if your mate down the pub offered, you'd probably say no. Wherever your capability is low, there will be high risk. While you should be taking more risks, be aware of the difference between recklessly gambling with something you know little or nothing about and taking a measured risk after having learnt as much as you can. Invest in your learning, get to a point where you feel capable and confident, then take the risk. You will never get to a point where you know everything before you start so you can never eradicate risk altogether. But learning the basics before starting will significantly reduce your risk. In the next lesson, we will expand on this by planning for what might go wrong.

Lesson summary:

1. Loss-aversion means we feel the pain of loss twice as much as the pleasure of an equivalent gain.
2. Reframe your idea of safety: sitting on the sidelines is not safe, you risk losing out on opportunities for a better life.
3. Risk is inversely related to capabilities, increase your abilities to reduce your risk.

Lesson #70: Think about what could go wrong upfront

"You're always ready for anything that comes your way"
Michael Phelps

At the Beijing Olympics in 2008, moments before the 200 m butterfly final, Michael Phelps stood behind his starting block bouncing on his toes and swinging his arms in preparation for the race. As his name was called out, he stepped up onto the starting block, and waved to the crowd then got into his stance ready for the race to start. The gun fired and he dived into the pool. Phelps knew that something was wrong as soon as he hit the water. Water was leaking into his goggles, and he couldn't tell where the leak was coming from. As he began swimming, he hoped the leak wouldn't become too bad and completely fill his goggles with water. However, by the second turn, everything was blurry. As he approached the third turn and final length, water filled his goggles. Phelps couldn't see anything. He couldn't see the line on the bottom of the pool, the T marking the approaching wall, or how many strokes remained. For most swimmers, losing your sight in the middle of an Olympic final would put an end to any chance of winning.

Phelps remained calm. He was prepared for this scenario. His coach had once made him swim in the dark, believing that he needed to be ready for anything that could go wrong. In doing this, he had already rehearsed how he would respond to a goggle failure. As he started his last length, Phelps estimated how many strokes it would require. He started counting. He felt relaxed as he swam at full strength. At 18 strokes, he started anticipating the wall.

He could hear the crowd roaring. Since he was blind, he had no idea where he was in the race. Nineteen strokes, then twenty. It felt like he needed one more. He made the twenty-first stroke and glided with his arm outstretched and touched the wall. He had timed it perfectly. When he ripped off his goggles and looked up at the scoreboard, not only had he won the gold medal, but he'd also set a new world record.

Standing between you and what you want to achieve, there will always be obstacles and things will go wrong. Failure is an integral part of the process, but you can take steps to think about what could go wrong upfront. This way, you can take preventative action to reduce the frequency and extent of your failures or even eliminate them. At the very least, you can take obstacles in your stride when they do occur as they won't be unexpected.

Perform a risk assessment on your goals

As you work towards your goals, you will encounter risks to your success. The best way to address these obstacles is with a risk assessment. Risk assessment is the systematic approach for the identification, analysis, and control of events that may pose a risk. We can take the same approach in goal achievement using the well-established principles of risk management, by following the steps outlined below:

1. Risk identification

Identify all the obstacles standing between you and the achievement of your goals. This can be a difficult exercise to do upfront, especially when starting something for the first time which you know little about. Do your best to think about all potential sources. Ask yourself "What could go wrong as I work towards my goal?" Aim to write as many obstacles, problems, challenges, or failures as you can.

2. Risk analysis

For each identified risk, quantify how much risk the obstacle poses. To do this, use a technique known as Failure Mode Effect Analysis (or FMEA). Don't be put off by the name. This is a straightforward technique which answers the following questions:

   i. What is the probability it will go wrong?
  ii. What are the consequences if it does go wrong?
 iii. How likely is it that the risk will be detected if it does occur?

For each identified risk, give a score from 1-10 for:

   a. Probability of occurrence
     1. No chance of happening (0%)
     2. One in a thousand (0.01%)
     3. One in a hundred (1%)
     4. One in fifty (2%)
     5. One in twenty (5%)
     6. One in ten (10%)
     7. One in five (20%)
     8. One in four (25%)
     9. One in three (33%)
    10. One in two (50%)

b. Consequences
   1. No consequences
   2. Consequences are insignificant and require no action to correct
   3. Consequences cause a minor inconvenience
   4. Consequences will require a small amount of time/money/resource to correct
   5. Consequences are medium
   6. Consequences will require a larger amount time/money/resource to correct
   7. Consequences cause a major inconvenience
   8. Consequences will require addressing before any further progress can be made
   9. Consequences are significant and will cost a lot in time/money/resource to correct
   10. Consequences will put a stop to what you're trying to achieve

c. Ability to detect
   1. Can detect 100% of the time
   2. Can detect 80% of the time
   3. Can detect 75% of the time
   4. Can detect 66% of the time
   5. Can detect 50% of the time
   6. Can detect 33% of the time
   7. Can detect 25% of the time
   8. Can detect 20% of the time
   9. Can detect 10% of the time
   10. Cannot detect/foresee

When you have assigned a number to each, multiply all three scores together to give a Risk Priority Number. This determines the overall priority you should provide to the risk. The higher the number, the greater the risk and the more preventative action is required.

3. Risk control

Now that risks have been identified and quantified, the next stage is to consider what can be done to reduce or eliminate risks. Prevention is better than cure. Successful people are solution-oriented so ask "How can I solve this problem?" You are doing this; the only difference is you're thinking about the problem before it happens. By thinking in this way, you begin to become proactive rather than reactive to issues.

4. Risk review

As you start to gain more experience with the things that can go wrong and how your risk control is working, you can feed this information back into the risk assessment.

Lesson summary:

1. Between you and your goals, there will always be obstacles.
2. Think about what could go wrong upfront and take steps to minimise or eliminate them from happening.

Lesson #71: Write a commitment contract

"Commitment is doing the things you said you would do, long after the feeling you said them in has left" Jeff Olsen

So, you've decided you want to make a change in an area of your life, and the previous lessons have shown you how to leave your comfort zone and navigate through the fear zone. The second 'C' in the confidence formula will ensure you stick with it long enough to make a sustained change. This is commitment. Commitment is such a commonly used word that we don't ever stop to think about what it means. When planning this lesson, there were a few basic questions I wanted to answer to clarify my thinking on commitment. Once I'd done this, I decided this was the best way to present this lesson, and so the following are those questions and answers.

What is commitment?

When you commit to something, you state how you intend to act towards that thing in the future. Commitment is, therefore, a personal promise to do what you say you'll do. It's your word. It's easy to make promises, but commitment makes sure you keep them and do what you said you would.

Why is commitment important?

Commitment means you continue working towards something long after the initial buzz has faded. You keep doing what you said you'd do, even when you don't feel like it. When things get tough, or you get bored, sticking to your commitment ensures you keep going long enough to create depth. *"Without commitment, you cannot have depth in anything whether it's a relationship, a business, or a hobby"* Neil Strauss. If you always stick to your commitments, the act of saying it means that whatever you're committing to has already happened, you just haven't made it a reality yet. *"Commitment is what transforms a promise into reality"* Abraham Lincoln.

What happens if I break a commitment?

There are two categories of commitments:

1. Commitment to others

   If you make a promise to do something for others and don't deliver what you said you would, you will lose their trust. If you did this in the business world, your reputation would go down the drain, and you'd have no customers and quickly be out of business. You are only as good as your word. Keep breaking it, and you will lose the trust and respect of others.

2. Commitment to yourself

   The same thing happens when you don't follow through on a commitment to yourself. You start to lose trust and respect in yourself. You say things like "I've quit before, so I'll quit again" and permit yourself to break the commitment. Do this too often, and you will eventually get to the stage where you stop making commitments because you know you won't follow through on them, so it's pointless making them.

   Breaking a commitment to yourself is like lying to yourself. You've said you'll do something, and you haven't followed through. You are the easiest person to lie to because no one is watching. You are only accountable to yourself. But know that if you do it once, you'll do it again. You're either all in and fully committed or not in at all. You can't commit some of the time and not others.

I always break my commitments. What can I do?

Complete a commitment contract to hold yourself accountable:

1. Write down what you are committing to. This is crucial as it makes it real. Write the words "*I commit to…*" then insert your promise. It can be anything you want. Once you've set your goals, you can make specific commitments to each of them.

2. Make as many commitments as you feel comfortable with but be realistic because once you've made these commitments in writing, you must stick to them. There is absolutely no room for compromise. If you compromise once, you'll do it again. Think of this as a contract with yourself, and it is not something you can break.

3. Underneath your commitments write out the declaration:

   I, <Insert name>, will keep the commitments listed in this contract. I am all in and I give myself completely to my commitments. There is no other option than to keep working towards them. However I feel, I will not compromise. I respect myself and my dreams to follow *through on the promises I make to myself. I will always show up for myself. In signing this contract, I agree to make these commitments binding.*

4. Sign it, date it, and keep it somewhere visible.

Now that you've made a firm commitment to do something, you've given yourself to it completely. There is no other option. The only choice from then on is to do what you say you'd do and follow through. A smart way to do this is to book an event, pay for it, and tell everyone you know. For example, one of my goals was to complete a triathlon so six months before the event, I booked my place.

Refer to your commitment contract every morning when you wake up and every night before you go to sleep. If the change is something you truly desire, respect yourself enough to follow through on the promises you make.

Lesson summary:

1. Commitment is a promise to do what you say you will do and will ensure you keep working towards your goals, even when you don't feel like it.
2. Break a commitment, and you will lose the trust and respect of others and yourself.
3. Write a commitment contract and refer to it daily.

Lesson #72: Create a personal curriculum

"A person who won't read has no advantage over one who can't"
Mark Twain

The final C in the confidence formula is capability. We live in the information age where there's a premium for knowledge and skills. The more you can acquire, the more valuable you become. There's more information available now than at any other time in human history. There's enough information to teach yourself any skill to achieve any goal. But the sad truth is that most people would rather level up their video game character than to level up themselves. You can no longer use the excuse you don't know how. Everything you need is out there. You just have to find it. If you believe that everything is learnable and make a commitment to lifelong learning, you are very well equipped to develop the capabilities to achieve the things you desire. This lesson explores some resources you can use to acquire the knowledge and skills needed. By the end, you will be able to write a personal learning plan.

Read

A few years ago, I discovered audiobooks. At the time, I was spending two hours a day commuting to and from work, so I started listening to them in the car. The average person in the UK drives 12,000 miles a year, which is equivalent to 300 hours behind the wheel, or two semesters studying. This is wasted time in which you can obtain the equivalent of a degree in subjects such as wealth building, success, sales, marketing, business, or any other topic simply by choosing to listen to books. You can also increase the speed of the reader, so I listen at 2x speed, meaning my 2 hours of listening becomes the equivalent of 4 hours reading time.

If you act on one thing from this book, start listening to audiobooks while doing something that doesn't require your full attention. You could be at the gym, gardening, cooking, or doing housework. If you can train your brain to listen on 2x times speed, just listening to half an hour per day equates to 50 books per year. This is in line with the number of books the average CEO will read. In comparison, the average adult reads less than one book per year. This simple, low-cost change to your life can massively separate you from the average.

Another thing to appreciate is that many of the authors are leaders in their fields. They are telling you how they achieved what they did, essentially giving you the answers. By reading their books, you have an insight into the minds of some of the world's most successful people, living and dead. What's exciting about this is you have access to them whatever your situation, for very little money. You can have any mentor you want if they have written a book. Take advantage of this valuable resource. If you want insight into the minds of people like Richard Branson or Alex Ferguson, pick up their books. Tai Lopez summarised it well with the following quote *"You need to start looking at books as mentors, not entertainment or educational resources. Treat them just like you would an in-person mentor. Some of the greatest mentors are no longer alive. But they are right there in your local library or available for practically free on Amazon. For just a few dollars, you have a network of mentors at your fingertips."*.

Books are one of the best, low-cost resources for learning

new skills. I have paid thousands of pounds to attend training courses, and the tutors have put the same content into their books which you can buy for a few pounds. The value you can get from a book is huge, so if you aren't regularly reading to increase your knowledge, you need to start now.

Mentors

If you want to become the best in your field, follow those that already are. Don't try to reinvent the wheel, just do what others have done, and you will be successful too – the formula is that simple. Copy everything about them, their behaviour, their dress sense, the books they read, the people they associate with, and their schedules. Follow the successful and success follows.

Top people are always willing to help others improve, but the reality is, they never get asked. It is not a negative attribute to ask for help. Identify people who are a few steps ahead of you and find out as much as possible from them. Don't ask Alan Sugar to be your business mentor if you're only just starting. Instead, ask friends and family who have businesses or attend local business networking events. Get a roadmap from the right person. All the answers are known; all you must do is seek out the people who have them and ask.

Learning groups and clubs

It is said that you are the product of the five people you spend the most time with. If you surround yourself with negativity, you will struggle to stay motivated in pursuit of your goals. Being continuously told that you can't do something or ridiculed and laughed at, you will start to believe it. Give up these relationships or at the least, limit the time you spend around these people. Instead, surround yourself with people that push you to do better, and you will have an endless supply of encouragement, emotional support, insight, accountability, and solutions. No drama or negativity, just increased motivation, achievement and bringing out the best in each other. Being around similar minded people who are working towards the same goals as you can be the difference between making it or not. If you want to start running, join a running club. Want to start reading more, join a book club. Whatever you want to do, there will be a club or group somewhere already doing it. And if there isn't, start your own.

Training courses

Training courses can be one of the best ways to learn new skills and knowledge; however, they do come at a price. When starting, much of what you will need can be found in books, however if you identify one essential skill or area that will have an enormous impact on your chances of success, you might decide that the cost is worth it. Remember that you are your best asset, and an investment today could pay dividends for many years to come. Rather than seeing the price of a training course as a cost, think of it as an investment in yourself.

Bringing it together in a curriculum

Bring all the above together in a simple one-page personal curriculum. At the top of the page, list the subject of interest.

Look to the future and identify the skills and knowledge required to achieve your goals and write these in as the learning objectives. Research books to read around the subject and look for suitable mentors and leading experts. Think about how you can gain access to them and material from them. Attend networking events and research clubs that you could join. These could be local groups where you physically attend events or internet groups. Look into and attend training courses to develop specific skills and technical knowledge.

Don't be afraid to spend some money. It can feel like you're wasting money because you don't see an immediate return on your investment. But over the long term, investing in your skills and knowledge is one of the best things you can do. Start by investing a minimum of 3% of your income into your personal and professional development. This is the figure that most successful companies use to invest in training for their staff so it should be the benchmark for you. Consistently reinvest 3% into yourself, and you will soon start to level up your life.

Lesson summary:

1. There's enough information available to learn any skill or knowledge required to achieve anything you want.
2. Identify the information you require to build a personal curriculum including books, training courses, mentors or learning groups.

Lesson #73: *When* you work is as important as *how* you work

"Time is what we want most but what we spent worst" William Payne

Time management is an essential skill for getting stuff done. It is ultimately the stuff that you get done (productivity) that will determine your success. Time management and productivity are the final two subjects of this chapter which we will explore over the remaining lessons.

Beneath the surface of our everyday life is a hidden pattern. The pattern is a peak followed by a trough then a rebound to a second peak. This pattern represents your productivity cycles throughout the day. To understand more about this pattern, we need to go back to 1729. French astronomer Jean de Mairan observed that the leaves of the *Mimosa pudica* plant closed at night and opened in the day. It inspired Mairan to experiment with the plant. He placed it in a dark box overnight and to his surprise, when he took the plant out of the box the following morning, the leaves were open despite still being in complete darkness. The plant wasn't responding to the light in its external environment but to its internal clock.

Since then, scientists have discovered that all living things have internal biological clocks or circadian rhythms. The result of these rhythms is that, like the *Mimosa pudica* plant, humans metaphorically open and close during certain parts of the day. Knowing these patterns, you can make sure you do your most important work when you're "open" as this is when you perform best.

Understand your chronotype

Although the same peak, trough, peak pattern is found in most of us, we don't all experience this at the same time of the day. We each have what is known as a chronotype, and this dictates the times of day you will experience your peaks and troughs. In simple terms, a morning person will experience their peak in the morning, the trough in the afternoon, and a second peak in the late afternoon/ early evening. A night owl will experience the same pattern except their first peak will be late morning/early afternoon, their trough in the late afternoon or early evening, and their second peak late at night. Your chronotype depends on several factors including genetics, sex, and even the time of year you were born but most noticeably, your age. Young children are morning people, teenagers are night owls reaching peak owl-age at 20 and slowly return to morning people over the rest of their lives.

To help you understand your chronotype, think about days when you don't have to wake up and ask yourself what time you usually go to sleep and wake up. Below shows an illustration of your daily performance pattern. Assume you wake-up at the T0 point on the diagram and go to sleep at T16.

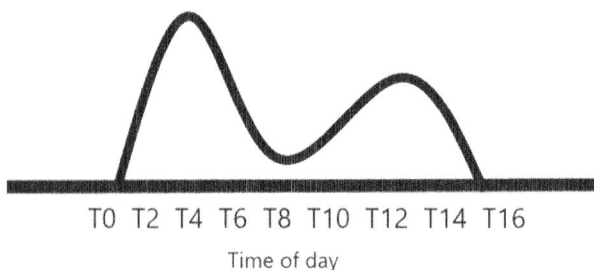

T0 T2 T4 T6 T8 T10 T12 T14 T16
Time of day

With a basic knowledge of your chronotype and the daily pattern, you can begin to schedule your day to align tasks with your peak times of the day. You can do your most important work in the first peak and second most important into the rebound period. Less important, mundane and admin tasks can be for your trough period. The result of organising your day in this way is increased productivity.

Figure out your daily "when" with the following steps:

1. Determine your chronotype by thinking about when you go to sleep and wake up
2. Determine your peak, trough, and rebound times. Track your behaviour systematically for a week. Set your phone alarm to go off every hour, and each time it does ask you're the following questions:
    i. What are you doing?
    ii. On a scale of 1-10, how mentally alert do you feel right now?
    iii. On a scale of 1-10, how physically energetic do you feel right now?
3. Determine the task you need to do. Does it require you to be mentally alert, or is it a mundane admin task?
4. Look at your daily "when" chart to figure out the optimal time of day for the task. Schedule essential tasks that require most of your mental and physical energy for peak times. Schedule tasks that don't need much energy for the trough.

Lesson summary:

1. We all experience the day in three stages: a peak, a trough and a rebound period.
2. Exactly when we experience these during the day depends on your chronotype.
3. Determine the tasks that need to be completed in the day: schedule your most important work during your peak, your second most important work during your rebound and the mundane and admin tasks during your trough.

Lesson #74: Schedule low-value activities in the afternoon

"Our little pebble of poor performance helps to start, or to sustain, an avalanche" Neal Maxwell

To illustrate the effect the afternoon has on your performance and why you should schedule low-value activities then, this lesson explores some studies done in hospitals at various times of the day.

The effect the afternoon has on performance:

1. Patients treated in the afternoon are three times more likely to receive a fatal dose of anaesthetic and considerably more likely to die within 48 hours of surgery when compared with those treated in the morning.
2. Gastroenterologists find fewer polyps during colonoscopies, so cancerous growths go undetected. One study of more than 1,000 colonoscopies found that endoscopists are less likely to detect polyps as the day progresses. Every hour that passed resulted in nearly a

5% reduction in polyp detection. At 11 am, doctors found an average of 1.1 in every exam, by 2 pm only half that amount were detected.

3. Interns are 26% more likely to prescribe unnecessary antibiotics for viral infections, thereby contributing to antibiotic resistance.

4. Nurses and caregivers are less likely to wash their hands before treating patients, increasing the probability that patients will contract an infection in the hospital. One study looking at the handwashing habits of 4,000 caregivers covering a total of 14 million opportunities to wash hands found there was a 38% decline in the afternoon. Researchers wrote *"The decrease in handwashing we detected in a typical work shift would contribute to approximately 7,500 unnecessary infections per year, at an annual cost of approx. $150 million across the 34 hospitals included in this study"*. Extrapolating this across the whole of the US equates to 600,000 unnecessary infections, $12.5 billion costs, and up to 35,000 unnecessary deaths.

The afternoon is a dangerous time to be a patient due to significantly reduced performance. So, what can we do when most of us are required to work in the afternoon? Be aware of this lull in productivity and schedule low-value activities that require little care and attention.

Lesson summary:

1. Avoid essential tasks in the afternoon and instead, schedule low-value activities that require less care and attention.

Lesson #75: Don't wish you had more time, instead take on less

"Time is slipping away for all of us at the same pace. You cannot manage time, but you can manage your energy" Sadhguru

We all have busy lives and wonder how we'll find the time to focus on what is important to us. There are only so many hours in the day, and with work and family commitments, it leaves little time for you. With what remains, you're probably too tired to do anything meaningful. You wish you had more time to achieve all the things you'd hoped for. So, in the end, all those things just become wishes instead of plans. Understanding how to manage your time is one of the most useful skills you can learn. When you do, you know what the best use of your time is. You can say no to the unimportant stuff that competes for your time. You use time with intention and work on things that will get you to where you want to go.

Almost every book I have read on increasing productivity has been based around time management and so to increase your output, you must have better control over how you spend your time. However, rather than focus your energy on time management, look to improve your personal management. Let me explain. You cannot manage time; it will tick along whatever you choose to do. But you can manage yourself. You are free to choose your actions and how you spend your time.

If you're reading this thinking, I simply don't have enough time, use the following technique to change your attitude towards time. Never say "I don't have enough time" because when you say this, you focus on the part that you have no control over. We all have 24 hours; you cannot slow down time or make more of it. By saying, "I don't have enough time", you create an image in your mind that you are helpless because you can't create more time. Your focus is on the one part you can do absolutely nothing about. Instead, focus on what you can control. And that is the amount of 'stuff' we want to do within a given timeframe. Instead, say "I've taken on more than can be done in the time available". You are in control of the amount of stuff you take on, and the remedy is quite simple. Take on less.

Lesson summary:

1. Time management is personal management.
2. Reframe "I don't have enough time" to "I've taken on more than can be done in the time available" and take on less.

Lesson #76: Place your rocks in the jar first

"Time isn't the main thing, it's the only thing" Miles Davis

A philosophy professor once filled a jar with large rocks and asked his class whether the jar was full. The students said yes. He then added small pebbles in the gaps around the rocks and asked once again. The students again replied that it was full. The professor then filled the jar with sand and asked for a final time whether the jar was full. The rocks, pebbles, and sand signify the things in your life. The most efficient way to fill the jar is with the large objects first. The reason for this is if you tried putting the sand in first, you wouldn't fit the same number of pebbles or rocks in.

Take the same approach when you manage your time. You must start allocating time to those things which always use up a fixed amount of time (your rocks). Once you have done this, you know what time you have left for the things which are more flexible (your pebbles and sand). For example, using the 168 hours in a week, you might allocate your time in the following way:

Hours asleep (rock): 56; 112 hours remaining

Hours at work (rock): 40; 72 hours remaining

Hours travelling (rock): 7; 65 hours remaining

Hours exercising (pebble): 7; 58 hours remaining

Hours relaxing (pebble): 14; 44 hours remaining

Spare hours for other tasks (sand): 30; 14 hours remaining

Time left for your goals (sand): 14 hours

Think about how you spend a typical week and what things are fixed and cannot be changed. Allocate some of your time to these activities and work out what time you have left. Next are the things that are important to you however are more flexible. For example, going to the pub. This is not something that you have to do but still is something that uses some of your time allocation. Again, subtract this time from your weekly total. The time you have left is your spare time. This is the time you can use to work on yourself and your goals. If you find that you don't have any spare time left, you will need to recover some time from your pebble activities and we will look at this in the next lesson.

Lesson summary:

1. Fill your time with large rocks first, then pebbles and sand.

Lesson #77: There is life beyond your day job

"If you live for the weekends and vacation, your shit is broken" Gary Vaynerchuk

Millions of people are living for the weekend or their next paycheck, trapped in the cycle of work, spend, work, making little time for their priorities. Most aren't conscious enough to even be aware that they are serving someone else's vision and for those who are, the feeling of being trapped by the paycheck means they never take action for a better life. Don't wish your life away counting down to the next weekend or paycheck. There is another way: start living with intention. Design your life plan because the reality is, if you're not working to your plan, you're working to someone else's. Even if you get paid well, you are limiting yourself because you're exchanging your time for money and you can't generate more hours in the day. You must start working hard for yourself. This doesn't mean quit your job tomorrow, only that you should be dedicating some of your spare time working towards your dreams and aspirations.

Beyond the typical 9-5 work hours, you have a day within a day that you can use to work on your own thing. If you have a 9-5 job which doesn't fulfil you, you have another 8 hours in the day to change that. Don't work 8 hours for a company then go home and not work on your own goals. We are all too willing to work hard for someone else for 40 years, so why not start working hard for yourself? The most confusing human logic is saying "It's too risky or takes too much effort or money to set out a plan for achieving my goals and dreams". You are effectively saying "I will stay in the safe and secure job that I hate for the next 40 years, live for the weekend, hate every Monday of my life and never explore my potential so I can die having been miserable and unsatisfied for decades. On the plus side, at least I won't have risked losing any time or money". The reality is you're already wasting so much time doing things like watching TV and spending money on rubbish you don't need, neither of which bring you much, if any, fulfilment. Use that time and money on your development and goals.

Don't say that you're tired from work. You're not tired, you're just uninspired. If you have a clear enough picture of your vision and a strong enough will to make it happen, then you'll find the energy to work on yourself. You must make deliberate use of your time outside of work; otherwise, you'll default to whatever catches your attention or whatever is easiest.

We all have the choice of how we spend our free time. You can waste it watching hours of Netflix, partying at weekends and sleeping in all morning. Or you can wake up early, exercise, read books and learn new skills that will enable you to grow into the person you want to become. How you spend your spare time is one of the best indicators of where you'll be in the future.

If there's one single thing you can do now that will free up time, it's throw away your TV. Depending on the source, on average, people watch between 4-6 hours of TV every day. When you stack up this time over a longer period, the amount of time you waste is enormous. This is 28-42 hours a week, 112-168 hours per month, or 1,344-2,016 hours per year. That means you lose one week out of every month or 12 weeks a year watching TV. Over 85 years of life, this equates to 20 years of your life sitting in front of your TV! That's an insane amount of time wasted. If someone offered you another 20 years of life, you'd bite their hand off for it. Well, this is entirely within your control today. Think about what you could achieve if you invested that time in your development. You could still live the same life you do now, but instead of watching TV, you respect yourself enough to give that time back to yourself. If you can't stand the thought of never watching Love Island again, try halving the amount of time you spend watching it and give yourself the other half. You need to start investing some of the time you waste into yourself, your goals, and your dreams. It may not be the TV that steals your spare time from you. It could be social media. Whatever it is, the issue is that we aren't aware of how we spend our time. If you raise your awareness by doing the exercise in the previous lesson, it can make you think twice about how you end up using it.

Lesson summary:

1. Don't wish your life away counting down to the next weekend or paycheck.
2. Design your spare time so that you work towards your vision.

Lesson #78: Leverage other people's time

"I would rather earn 1% off a 100 people's effort than 100% of my own efforts" John D. Rockefeller

All of the world's most successful people have achieved what they have with the same number of hours in a day as you and I. Yet they have achieved so much more, and this is because they have mastered the skill of leveraging other people's time. There is one point, in particular, I would like to mention in this lesson. If adopted, it can help change your mindset towards leveraging other people and fast-track your progress.

Work out what your hourly wage is. Next, think about all the low-value activities you do in a week, for example, clean your car or iron your shirts. If the hourly cost of getting someone else to do those low-value tasks is less than what you can earn in an hour, then you should be outsourcing them. For example, imagine you make £30 an hour and to pay for someone to clean your car costs £10. You might think that by washing your car yourself, you're saving yourself £10, but this is costing you an hour of your life. You could have spent that hour working, earnt £30 and have a net gain of £20. Or to put it another way, you could have worked for 20 minutes to earn the £10 to clean your car then spent the remaining 40 minutes on something more important. Your most precious resource is time. So, work out what your time is worth and never exchange it for anything worth less. Other people can work for you to free up your time for the more important things.

Lesson summary:

1. Leverage other people's time if their time is worth less than your hourly rate.

Lesson #79: Make your schedule your servant, not your master

"Either run the day or the day runs you" Jim Rohn

It's time to start using the knowledge from the last few lessons to design a schedule to work on what matters most. To help you do this, follow the steps below:

1. The first thing is to track where you spend your time over an average week. Set your alarm to go off every hour that you're awake and write down what you're doing. You can choose to block off large chunks of time for work, for example, or you might be interested to see how you spend your time during those working hours too. You can be as detailed as you like.
2. After a week of tracking your time, analyse your results. Highlight where you waste time or do low-value tasks. The point of this is to prove to yourself that you have more time than you think. If you're brutally honest, you should be able to find a spare 1 or 2 hours each day. This is like finding free money and is time you can spend on your goals. Unless you reserve this time for yourself, it will slip by.
3. Remind yourself of the take-home messages from the previous few lessons, and keep these in mind when you start designing your schedule:

a. Understand your chronotype and productivity peaks and troughs
b. Schedule your most important work first
c. Schedule low-value activities in your trough period
d. Schedule other important tasks during the rebound period
e. Take on less
f. Schedule large immovable things first
g. Work outside of work
h. Leverage time by using other people

4. Start by entering your large, immovable rocks first. For this, enter things like sleep, work, and other commitments that you cannot move.

5. Once you have your big rocks in the jar, schedule 1 to 2 hours a day to work on your own goals. Aim to do this during your peak periods and aim to do this in at least 1-hour blocks. Make sure you can fully focus and eliminate any distractions. You might also find that you have small pockets of time of 15 minutes throughout your week that you can make use of. These can add up to be significant chunks of time over a few years.

6. Finally, schedule in your downtime activities such as watching TV or whatever else you do to relax.

You should now have a better understanding of where you spend your time and how you can set some time aside for working on your goals and dreams. It's easy to ignore these things and allow external demands to control your time. Scheduling your essential work ahead of time will ensure you get it done. Now you can take back control of your time, be intentional with it, and use it for the things that are truly important to you. You can leave the distracted masses and join the focused few actively working towards a better life. Treat time with the respect it deserves because once you've spent it, it's gone forever. Where you choose to spend your time, your life will follow.

Lesson summary:

1. Create a schedule that works for you.

Lesson #80: Pull the CORD

"For every minute spent in organising, an hour is earned" Benjamin Franklin

This lesson provides details of the system I use for organising and doing all of my work both in my personal life and professional life. CORD is the acronym for capture and collect, organise, review and do. It comes from the book *How to be a Productivity Ninja* by Graham Allcott. This system is the one I have found easiest to use as it takes in everything you need to do and ensures you complete it. If you adopt this system (or something similar) and integrate the habit into your life, it will transform how you get stuff done.

When we get thrown stuff from every angle, it can be overwhelming and stressful. It is easy to forget important tasks which down the line means you're putting out fires and being reactive and this further compounds the stress. Before long, it can feel like you're drowning in your work with no hope of ever getting on top of it again. With the CORD system, you can be confident that you have captured everything, have given it sufficient thought, and that the things you choose to do will be the most effective use of your time.

The system removes the most unreliable part of the process – you. You're notoriously unreliable, and if you rely on your memory alone, you will forget things. Instead, pass on that responsibility to CORD, let it do most of the thinking for you. You only have to remember a few key things about how to operate the system.

When working through the steps below, think of your brain as having two main parts:

1. The worker part – this is the part that wants to receive specific instruction and crack on with the task, it doesn't want to think.
2. Leader part – this part wants to do all the thinking, planning, and strategy but not get involved with the day-to-day work. The leader generates instructions for the worker.

Each part has its role in the CORD system, and you need to be fully aware of which part is engaged in each step. During a standard day, we will frequently switch between the leader and worker modes and this is very inefficient. Instead, by following the CORD system, you will engage the leader modes at particular times to organise your work schedule, then most of the day you will be in worker mode doing the work. This way, you can do all your boss work at defined times, then have the freedom to get on and do the work for the remaining time. By carefully planning, you won't have to waste valuable brain power switching between leader and worker modes during the day, you simply trust that your leader brain has prepared your day and crack on with the work.

The CORD system

1. Capture and collect, worker brain engaged

How many times have you had a good idea or thought of something you need to do but later forgot about it? It's estimated that we have approximately 65,000 thoughts per day, so if you rely purely on your brain to remember everything for you, you'll almost certainly fail. So often, I would think of a good idea for this book but didn't capture it straight away and later forgot about it. The capture and collect phase removes this problem as it acts as a funnel for every possible source of input. There are two rules for this part of the process.

The first is capture everything. The point of this part of the process is to ensure nothing gets missed. It's completely uncensored and requires no thinking or filtering. Just because you capture everything, does not mean you commit to doing it all. Don't try to sort or prioritise at this stage; the rejection and organising process starts at the next step. As no thinking is required, this step involves your worker brain. Sources of inputs can include, for example, your thoughts, your emails, your friends and family, your boss, your work colleagues, anything which requires you to progress the task.

The second key part of the process is to remove yourself from having to remember anything. In other words, capture immediately. The only way to consistently achieve this is to capture things the moment they come to you. If you rely on your memory, there's a good chance that you'll miss something. You, therefore, need a simple and easy way to capture all these inputs. I would suggest using the notes app or other similar to-do list apps on your phone or a pen and paper. Remember that if you have a variety of capture methods, you need a process of bringing all the inputs together. Your "in-tray" should be filled with lots of things. Get everything out of your brain and into a system you can trust to deal with it.

2. Organise, leader brain engaged

During the organising stage, careful thought is required so you must engage your leader brain. To avoid switching between leader and worker mode too often, I would suggest spending an hour or two once or twice a week to focus on organising new inputs. During this part of the process, you take your inputs from step 1 and file them into one of the following:

i. Projects – this is the high-level category. They are a collection of tasks designed to achieve a particular aim, for example, your long-term goals. The point of making a project list is to spend a few short moments each week, gaining clarity on the bigger picture. I have a projects list which has the headers "Planned", "In-progress" and "Complete". This acts as a conveyer belt for projects, and as they progress, they move through the various stages.

After 6-12 months, the completed projects drop off the list.

ii. Master actions list – this list contains every single action you could do for each task and project. It is action-focused, so each action should describe precisely what you need to do next. Your worker self needs very specific instructions. It can't think. The job of your leader self is to take the input from the capture and collect stage and set very specific actions for your worker self. Your action list should be full of things that your worker brain can read, and which provides sufficient instruction to crack on without giving any thought to them. To be specific, an action must contain a verb (the action you want to perform, e.g. read), an object (the thing that has an action performed on it, e.g. a book) and a subject (the thing performing the action). In the example, "I will read a book on investing", read is the verb, the book is the object, and I am the subject.

3. Review, leader brain engaged

This is broken down into two key parts: the longer weekly review and the shorter 5-minute daily review before the start of each day. I would recommend doing the weekly review immediately after the weekly organise.

i. Stages of weekly review:
   a. Remove actions from the Master Actions List that have been completed that week.

b. If new actions result from the completed ones, write these onto the Master Action List.

c. If the action is the last one required to complete a project, move that project from the "In-progress" column to the "Complete" column.

d. Promote a project from the "Planned" column up to the "In-progress column".

ii. The daily checklist – 5 minutes at the start of the day, engage your leader brain to choose actions from your Master Actions List. The daily checklist will separate thinking from doing. Your leader brain will do the thinking, write the checklist, and give it to your worker. Your worker self is given such clarity on what to do, the only decision is when not how. You should be able to answer this question from the previous lessons in this chapter. Ask yourself five questions in 5 minutes at the start of each day when looking at your Master Action List:

a. What's in my calendar today and are there any deadlines looming in the next 3-5 days?

b. What are the 2-3 significant actions that require focus today?

c. From those tasks, which am I likely to resist wanting to do and why? Move it to first on your list.

d. From those tasks, which require the most attention?

e. Are any actions dependent on time, people, or resources?

Once done, pull actions from your Master Actions Lists for the day. I tend to highlight these actions on the list and when complete, will strikethrough them.

4. Do, worker brain engaged

Doing should be the easiest step because, by the time you get to it, all the hard work is done. You simply follow the instructions your leader brain has given you.

It may seem counterintuitive that if you spend more time thinking about your work, rather than just doing it, that you'll be more productive, but I promise you I have found this to be the case. As the saying goes, it's better to measure twice and cut once so the extra time you spend planning will pay off. After adopting this system, I would estimate that my productivity has doubled despite me spending 3-4 hours a week extra planning the work. Try it.

Lesson summary:

1. Don't rely on your memory alone to organise your work, use a system to do most of the work for you.
2. Capture everything and capture it immediately.
3. Organise and review your workload weekly with your leader brain.
4. Use your leader brain to set up daily work for your worker brain to do.

7 THE MIDDLE
MONITOR PROGRESS

The mid-point is often the hardest part of the process. We're highly motivated and energised at the start and when the end is near, this provides the drive to push on and finish strong. But the middle is the long slog. The motivation you had at the start has dwindled, and you're still so far from the end that you can't see the light at the end of the tunnel. Because of this, we tend to relax our standards in the middle. But if we're aware of this, we can prepare for the challenges that arise at the mid-point and take steps to reduce the consequences. We will explore these challenges in this chapter and discuss how you can overcome them and stay motivated until the end.

Lesson #81: Evolve with punctuated equilibrium

"The whole point of being alive is to evolve into the complete person you were intended to be" Oprah Winfrey

Charles Darwin proposed that evolution was a slow and gradual process, in which a species accumulated small variations over long periods. However, if evolution's path was a smooth, linear progression, then there should be fossils showing these small incremental changes to the new species. But in many cases, scientists have been unable to find most of these intermediate fossils.

In 1972, evolutionary scientists Stephen Jay Gould and Niles Eldredge proposed another explanation which they called punctuated equilibrium. That is, species are generally stable, changing little for millions of years. This leisurely pace is "punctuated" by a rapid burst of change that results in a new species. The actual trajectory of evolution is, therefore, thought to be much less linear. This is just one of many examples in nature that shows progress is not linear.

Another example is the Chinese bamboo tree. After sowing the seed, the ground is watered and fertilised in the first year, but nothing happens. It's watered and fed again in the second, and nothing happens. Again, in the third and fourth years but still, nothing happens. Then in the fifth year, the tree grows roughly 90 feet in the space of six weeks. But this tree didn't grow 90 feet in 6 weeks. It took five years of careful preparation to grow to this height. Had the ground not been watered or fertilised during one of the first four years, it would not have grown.

Both evolution and the Chinese bamboo tree teach us a valuable lesson about progress in life. You may experience long periods where it feels as though you aren't making the progress you'd like. Don't allow this to frustrate you or get you down. With the knowledge that progress isn't linear, you can remain motivated even when results don't come. You know that if you keep working, you will eventually punctuate this equilibrium and experience significant breakthrough moments.

If you were to plot your progress on a chart, it would look something like the right-hand chart below. The graph of the left shows the type of progression most people expect.

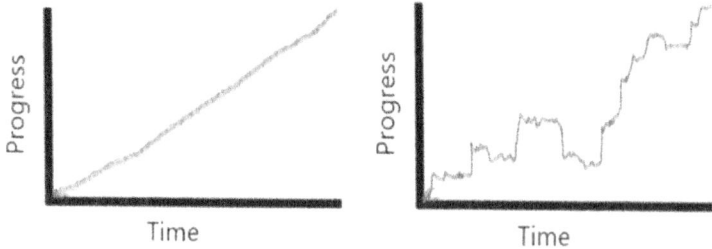

The important thing to remember is that if you can still reach your destination in the desired timeframe, the shape of your graph doesn't matter. Whether it's the nice smooth linear progression you want it to be or the progress shown on the right-hand chart, the key thing is you reach your end goal in the same timeframe. The only thing you have to overcome is your psychology. The way to do this is simply be aware that progress will come in bursts. Expect it to follow this pattern, and you won't be disheartened when you feel like you're not making the progress you want. Keep working, and you'll reach your end goal.

Lesson summary:

1. Progress is not linear; you will experience periods where you make little or no progress followed by breakthrough moments.
2. The pattern of your progress is not important, all that matters is where you end up.

Lesson #82: Honour the struggle

"Adversity introduces a person to themselves" Albert Einstein

We live in a time of convenience, where everything is designed to make life easier for us. With society continually telling us to do what is easy, why would we choose to take the hard option? Most of us will actively avoid struggle. Yet not one successful person who has achieved great things managed to do so without struggle. So why should it be any different for you? Struggle is a natural part of life; a chick must struggle out of its shell to live. Yet as soon as things get difficult for us, we quit. People often leave jobs, businesses, and marriages at the first sign of difficulty. You need to stop seeing the struggle as a negative and start embracing it as a necessary part of the process for development and progress.

Without adversity, you don't have the opportunity to build character and cultivate resilience. So, if you're reading this thinking you have it easy, start manufacturing some struggle in your life. Choose the hard option, however, small the task. Take the stairs instead of the lift. Walk to the shop instead of driving. Whenever faced with a decision between an easy option and a hard option, take the hard one. This will help you better deal with life's basic challenges before facing real challenges. It will start to transform your attitude towards adversity and also act as a stress inoculation, so when you face more important challenges, you won't cower away from them. Just as with fear, adversity is pointing the way to success. Instead of seeing it as a stop sign, follow it. It's a big arrow guiding you towards great things.

Lesson summary:

1. Reframe your attitude to adversity, view it as a necessary part of the process to success.
2. Manufacture some adversity in your life, always take the hard option to prepare you for bigger challenges down the line.

Lesson #83: Never give up

"Never give up on something that you can't go a day without thinking about" Winston Churchill

As you work towards your goals, at times, you will feel the urge to give up. You still have so far left to go, and you're low on energy and motivation. Your head will start to fill up with all the reasons why you should quit. But you must resist this as the rewards in life go to the person who never gives up. I've heard so many inspirational stories about people never giving up and fighting against all the odds to succeed. So many, that it was difficult to pick just one for this lesson. It could have been Danny Williams, a boxer who dislocated his arm and still managed to win the fight or Terry Fox, a 21-year old one-legged cancer patient who ran 3,339 miles across Canada in 143 days before dying. But it's the story of World War II medic, Desmond Doss, I find most inspiring.

The young medic singlehandedly saved the lives of 75 American soldiers on the Maeda Escarpment of Okinawa in 1945. Doss refused to carry a weapon, so when called to fight, he earned the title "conscientious objector". But instead of refusing to fight, Doss asked to work as a medic. The army resisted this for a while then begrudgingly gave him this role. His fellow soldiers mocked him for not having the bravery to fight. No one wanted to be his friend because he couldn't look out for them without carrying a weapon.

Then came the battle at the Okinawa Maeda Escarpment, or what Americans called Hacksaw Ridge. It was 5 May 1945. It was a particularly grueling onslaught with artillery coming so fast that it was ripping men in half. The Japanese had waited until all the Americans reached the plateau before opening fire to inflict maximum devastation. In an act that still astounds the surviving members of his company, amidst never-ending gunfire and mortar shells, for hour after hour, Doss crawled and dragged each hurt member to the edge of the ridge and carefully lowered them down to safety. For more than 12 hours, Doss laboured under fire, refusing to leave a single man on top of the ridge. But the part of this story I find most inspirational happened two weeks later.

Doss was in battle again when a Japanese grenade landed in his trench, where he was treating a soldier. He attempted to kick the grenade away, but it detonated, leaving him with deep shrapnel lacerations in his legs. He treated himself for shock and dressed his wounds rather than having another medic emerge from safety to treat him. Five hours later, a stretcher arrived, but as soon as Doss saw a soldier in need, he rolled off, surrendered his stretcher, and started patching up his comrade. While waiting for help to arrive, a sniper shot and shattered all the bones in Doss's left arm. Doss then crawled 300 yards with severely injured legs and a broken arm to the aid station. Put yourself in his shoes during those moments as he crawled with grenade shrapnel in his legs and bullet fragments in his injured arm. He refused to give up, despite the incredible risk to his life and the massive injury to himself. He was awarded a Medal of Honour for his bravery and heroism, the first "conscientious objector" to do so.

When I read this story, it put my excuses into context. Ask yourself *"What is my excuse for giving up?"* Are you too tired? Don't have enough time? Or money? Recognise that the excuses you keep telling yourself are not valid. The truth is you have everything you need right now to get it done. You've done a lot of the hard work in getting to this point. Don't throw that all away now because of an excuse you're telling yourself. You need to fight for anything worthwhile in life. It's not going to fall in your lap. It's always going to be difficult. You have to resist all the excuses you tell yourself. If you want it, you've got to go and get it. This is your moment. Never give up.

Lesson summary:

1. You will feel the urge to give up as you work towards your goals.

2. Fight this urge by taking inspiration from stories of those who have faced tougher challenges than you and didn't give up.
3. Your excuses are not valid; you have everything you need to get it done.

Lesson #84: Learn to deal with boredom

"The opposite of happiness isn't sadness, it's boredom" Tim Ferris

However much you love what you do and however strong your passion is, at some point, you will face boredom. And this will probably come during the mid-point. But what exactly is boredom, and how can we learn to better deal with it? In this lesson, we will try to answer those questions.

Boredom is the experience of not being able to engage in an activity which you find satisfying. Some of the tasks you must do in service of your longer-term goals will involve repetition. Any experience which is predictable and repetitive can become monotonous and boring. A top athletics coach was asked what it takes for someone to become an athlete and he replied by saying *"At some point, it comes down to who can handle the boredom of training every day"*. You too must learn to handle boredom.

Most people want to feel motivated before they decide to work on their goals, even if it's something they enjoy doing. People speak of being passionate about what they do, and this passion being their driving force. But successful people feel the same boredom and lack of motivation as everyone else. The difference between them and the rest of us is that they work despite these feelings. They don't let their emotions determine their actions. They know they have set the right goals, and if they continue to work and push through the boredom, they will get their reward.

The way to work through the boredom is to gain clarity on your core values, vision, and purpose. When you know these things, you know that your current actions align with them and are contributing in a significant way to your longer-term vision. If you do the exercises in this book, boredom shouldn't be a strong enough force to knock you off path. Only those who are working on something without understanding why can be disrupted by boredom. These people will try something new, do it for a while, then get bored and try something else. I know this because I used to do the same thing. I would go through fads of doing something for a few months then get bored and trying something else. But as soon as I took the time to get clear on my core values, vision and why, my actions became more focused and intentional. The boredom I sometimes feel does not affect my willingness to work because I know I'm working towards something meaningful. Boredom comes some days, but I work anyway.

Lesson summary:

1. Any repetitive task can become tedious, so you will face boredom as you work towards your goals.
2. To work through boredom, get clear on your core values, vision and purpose and know that your current actions are contributing in a significant way towards those things.

Lesson #85: Don't break the chain

"Success isn't always about greatness. It's about consistency. Consistent hard work leads to success. Greatness will come" Dwayne Johnson

Making progress is satisfying. But to know you're making progress, you have to measure your progress. Measuring your progress is possibly the single most motivating thing you can do. As you start to see a real positive change, you will begin to change your belief system and be inspired to take further action. This has a cascade effect, and before you realise, you've integrated positive new habits into your life. With the right habits, you're on the path to success. So, what can we do to tap into this power?

<u>Don't break the chain</u>

One of the best ways to monitor progress is with a visual measure as this provides clear evidence that you're making steps forward. Buy yourself a calendar, where each page is a month of the year and each day is a box a few centimetres across and a few centimetres down. Whatever you decide to work on, if you achieve something significant during the day, put a big red cross on your calendar for that day. If you manage to make it through the day without smoking, for example, you put a big red cross in the box for that day.

We love to receive instant feedback that we're on the right track and marking big red crosses on a calendar provides this. When we receive a signal that we're moving forward, we're motivated to continue down that path. If we have to wait to see results, it can be demoralising and can lead to giving up. For example, if you're goal is to lose weight, you have to change your behaviour for several weeks before you start to see results. As such, you can become frustrated and give up when you don't see the impact soon enough. The chain technique provides instant feedback to your brain while you wait for the real results to come. Each small win feeds your desire to continue.

Tracking can become its own form of reward too. For example, I check my investment accounts each month and track the balance on a spreadsheet. I also have a graph showing the upward direction of the overall balance. It is exciting to see this moving upwards and motivates me to continue investing money. I look forward to the first of every month to see how the investments are doing. Tracking is about giving yourself small wins. With each small success, you build a body of evidence to support the identity you desire, and before long, you will see yourself as the person you want to be.

Never miss two days

Life will inevitably get in the way, meaning you can miss a day and break the chain. You also need to take days off to recharge. Give yourself a free cross each week. The important thing is never to miss two consecutive days as you will lose momentum. I can't tell you how many times I started something new and it was going well for a month or two. Then I went away on holiday and completely lost momentum and eventually stopped. The best way to avoid this from happening is to make sure you never miss two consecutive days. The first mistake is never the one that ruins you. It's the spiral of repeated mistakes that follows. Missing one day happens, we have busy lives and need a day off. But when you miss two days, you start to form a new habit. Everyone can, and does, have a bad day, but winners rebound quickly, and they are back at it the next day. Lost days hurt you more than successful days help you. For every lost day (not including your day off each week), imagine this sets you back a week. Show up, even on your bad days.

Lesson summary:

1. Use a calendar to mark days when you complete something significant to create a chain.
2. The chain provides instant feedback to your brain that you're making progress while you wait for the real rewards to come.
3. Never miss two days.

Lesson #86: Measure the gain, not the gap

"Don't compare yourself to others. That's when you start to lose confidence in yourself" Will Smith

Most of us will have a vision of where we want to be and start there in our minds. When we see where we are today, we realise how far off we are and become demoralised. Every day, we feel as though we are behind schedule and will never make it. This constant feeling of being behind eventually leads to giving up.

We also like to look at those who are already where we want to be and use them as a measuring stick for our progress. It's the logical thing to do, but it means your focus is on the distance still to go. It is so important that you do not compare yourself to others. They are at a completely different stage in their journey to you so when you do this, you're comparing your chapter 1 to their chapter 20, which is not a fair comparison. This is one of the fastest ways to unhappiness. Just remember that you are at a completely different stage and focus on running your race.

Imagine you're climbing a mountain, but as you start to make progress, you look up to see that the summit is still so far away. This is utterly demoralizing as your focus is on how far remains. Instead, turn around and see how far you've come. When you do this, you realise what you've achieved up to that point, and it motivates you to continue.

The same is true for your long- and medium-term goal. Remember to stop and look back at how far you've come. Go back to where you were when you started working on the goal and think about what's changed so far. Perhaps your goal was to lose five stone and so far, you've lost two stone. Instead of focusing on the three stone remaining, look back and celebrate how far you've come already. Or if your goal were to run a marathon and you're only running half marathons, this is a massive achievement and significant progress when you couldn't even run a mile before. This will provide you with the motivation you need to take the next small step. And the next. Until one day, you look up at the summit of the mountain and realise you're already there.

Lesson summary:

1. Don't compare yourself with those already where you want to be; they are at a completely different stage in their journey.

2. As you work towards your goals, focus on how far you've already come, not how far remains.

Lesson #87: Take a break

"Almost everything will work again if you unplug it for a few minutes... including you" Anne Lamott

If you're anything like me, you want to be working at a million miles per hour always looking for the next thing to do. But it's so important to take a break. While stopping to recover might seem like a waste of time, overall, you'll achieve much more if you do. To achieve anything meaningful will take a long time and is, therefore, a marathon, not a sprint. Doing too much, too quickly will lead to burn out and giving up.

In Israel, two judicial boards are responsible for processing almost half of the countries parole requests. It is the job of individual judges to hear the prisoner's case and decide whether they should be released. Judges aspire to be rational and objective to meet justice based on the facts of the case and the law. However, they're also human.

In 2011, social scientists studied data from the parole boards to examine judicial decision making. They found that early in the day, judges ruled in favour of prisoners about 65% of the time. As the morning wore on, that rate declined, and by late morning their favourable rulings dropped to zero. So, a prisoner slotted at 9.00 am was likely to be granted parole while one slotted at 11.45 am had very little chance regardless of the facts of the case. Immediately after the judges took a break, the decisions returned to being favourable. As the afternoon progressed, decisions became less favourable.

If you happen to appear before a parole board just before a break rather than just after, you'll likely spend a few more years in jail. Not because of the facts of the case but because of the time of the day. A factor that should have no bearing on justice, such as when the judge took a break, was critical in deciding whether someone would go free or not. This shows the importance of taking breaks and the effect they can have on your performance.

So, what can we do to integrate more frequent and more effective breaks into our day?

1. Take short breaks from a task – frequent short breaks are more effective than fewer longer breaks. Research by *Desk Time* has suggested a golden ratio of working for 52 minutes, followed by a 17-minute break. Make a "break list" by stating where you'll take breaks, how long they will be and what you're going to do.

2. Move – stand up and walk around for 5 minutes every hour. One study showed that short walks boosted energy levels, sharpened focus, improved mood, and reduced feelings of fatigue. They also increase motivation, concentration, and creativity. Get outside to maximise effects.

3. Fully detach – when you take a break, remove yourself from your work environment altogether and anything else that zaps your energy. Fully disconnect from your phone too.

4. Nap – research has shown the perfect nap is 10-20 minutes, combined with downing a cup of coffee just before, known as the Nappacino. By the time you wake up, the caffeine will be in your system, so you'll have a double pick-me-up. Anything longer than 20 minutes and you may experience sleep inertia and feel groggy. It takes the average person 7 minutes to nod off so factor this into your timings.

Lesson summary:

1. Remember that rest and recovery is vital if you want to maintain your efforts for long term success.
2. Take frequent, short breaks, aiming to stop work and detach yourself for at least 5 minutes every hour.

Lesson #88: Have an annual performance review

"You don't change your decision to go, but you do change your direction to get there" Zig Ziglar

As well as using the chain technique to monitor your daily progress, once in a while, you need to take a step back and assess where you are in the bigger picture of what you hope to achieve. An annual check-in will help ensure you're still on the right path. Just as you might have a yearly performance review at work, do this for your goals. This lesson will discuss how to review your performance and modify your goals to reflect changing priorities.

Spend a full day each year reviewing your goals. A good time to do this is at the end of the year. Your yearly review will go over all the things discussed in sections 1 and 2 of this book, so it can be helpful to re-read the lessons. The following steps should be part of your yearly review:

1. Think about whether you have any lingering limiting beliefs and attitudes, and if so, how can you work to overcome them? Revisit the lessons in chapters 1 and 2.

2. What habits have you adopted/changed over the last year which have made working on your goals easy? Are there any habits you've yet to adopt that you want to focus on in the next 12 months? If so, write these down and make plans to achieve them.

3. Review your vision and values. Have they changed over the last 12 months? Have the things you want changed? Revisit the lessons in chapter 4.

4. Think about why you are working on your goals. Are the reasons still valid?

5. Review your purpose statements. Are you living by them?

6. For any goals that you might have achieved, did you feel the way you expected to feel when you achieved them? If not, why not?

7. Think about your priorities. Do you need to say no to certain things right now so you can focus on particular actions?

8. For any new goals you've set throughout the year, have they been set using the rules in chapter 5?

9. When working on your goals, did you experience any resistance? If so, what and why do you think you experienced it? Understanding why can help you overcome it.

10. Have you experienced any obstacles or failures? If so, how did you feel about them at the time and how do you feel about them now? Did you overcome them and if so, how? What did you learn from them?

11. Review and update your curriculum. Review the learning you've done over the past year, what worked well for you and what didn't.

12. How much time have you been able to dedicate to your goals? Do you need to spend more or less time in one particular area of your life?

13. Are the systems you've implemented to get stuff done working well for you? Can any improvements be made to them?

14. How have you been tracking your progress? What has worked well for you?

15. Review your goals list from 12 months ago and consider the following outcomes:

    a. Rejoice - if you've reached a significant milestone, pause to recognise and celebrate it. Celebrating wins helps us stay emotionally engaged for the long haul and primes the brain's reward system, which helps you push on.

    b. Recommit - refocus on the original goal and reconnect with your why. List what is at stake, what will you gain, or what will you lose by not achieving it?

    c. Revise - when planning the original goal, you have limited knowledge. Does the knowledge you have today help you revise your goal for the better?

    d. Remove – if you can't recommit or revise, remove it. If it's no longer relevant or compelling, remove it.

    e. Replace – if you decide to remove a goal, try replacing with another. You should aim to maintain the same number of goals at any one time.

Lesson summary:

1. Spend a full day each year reviewing your goals.
2. Ask questions to review your performance over the past year.
3. Rejoice, recommit, revise, remove or replace your goals following the review.

Lesson #89: Use the Uh-Oh Effect to drive you to completion

"It always seems impossible until it's done" Nelson Mandela

Any sports fan will know that if their team is losing at half time, matching the opponent in the second half will guarantee defeat. The team ahead at half time has a higher probability of winning the game. However, there is an exception. A study analysing more than 18,000 NBA games over 15 years showed that there is a statistically higher chance of winning when you trail by one at half time. It was actually more advantageous than being up by one. Teams who were behind by one at halftime ended up winning 58% of the time. Statistically, it was equivalent to being ahead by 2 points. This phenomenon is explained by something called the 'Uh-Oh Effect'.

As we know from the first lesson in this chapter, progress is not linear. When we check our progress at the mid-point, we expect to be halfway towards our goal. But when realise we're behind where we "should" be, a mental alarm tells us that half our time is gone. As a result, we receive a hit of motivation to make up the gap. So, as you approach the mid-point and realise you've made little or no progress, the 'Uh-Oh effect' suddenly kicks-in and you press ahead as shown by the arrow of the diagram below.

Mid-points, therefore, provide the burst of motivation we need to drive on. The most motivating mid-point comes when you're running slightly behind. So, when you are checking in on the progress towards your goals, think about where you are and where you should be. Be aware of the mid-point 'Uh-Oh Effect' and use it to push on.

Lesson summary:

1. Being slightly behind where you expect at the mid-point can be an advantage as it will motivate you to act.

Mid-points are often the hardest part of the process. We're highly motivated and energised at the start, then when the end is in sight, this provides the drive to push on and finish strong. The middle part is the long slog. However, we can use the lessons in this chapter to prepare for the challenges that occur at the mid-point and take steps to prevent our standards slipping.

8 THE END
REACHING MY DESTINATION

Lesson #90: Finish with a sprint

"If you want a happy ending, it depends where you stop your story" Ernest Hemingway

The American psychologist, Clarke Hull, developed what he called the goal gradient hypothesis when observing rats in a maze. As the rats approached the goal (food), they moved at an increasingly rapid pace. We do something similar as we approach the end of our goals. The closer we get, the more energised we are to close the small gap that remains. It makes sense, as we see the finishing line approaching, we can give everything we have left to push to completion. This is seen in athletics when long-distance runners give everything in a sprint finish to the line. You can use whatever energy and resources you have remaining in the short distance that's left.

Another study looked into the number of points scored in the NFL between 2007 and 2017. It revealed that teams scored a total of 3,200 points more in the final minute than they scored in any other minute of the game, except the last minute of the first half (which is also an ending). Endings inspire us to sprint over the finish line. As I reached the end of this book, I wrote the last ten lessons in around a fortnight compared to the year it took to write the other 90. As soon as the end was in sight, it provided huge motivation to get over the finish line. As you approach the end of your goals, use the same force that motivated the rats to go faster and the American footballers to push harder and end with a sprint finish.

Lesson summary:

1. The goal gradient hypothesis states that as we approach the goal, we increase our effort to get over the finish line.
2. Give everything you have at the end.

Lesson #91: Define what success means to you

"What's money? A man is a success if he gets up in the morning and goes to bed at night and in between does what he wants to do" Bob Dylan

Throughout the book, we've used the word success to define what you're working towards. But what is success? Can you only claim you're successful when you've reached the end destination? Or can you be successful as you work towards it? In this lesson, we will try to answer these questions so you can be clear on what success means to you.

When you think of a successful person, what do you imagine? Chances are you see someone who is at the top of their field, has lots of money, lots of material items and is popular. This is what society defines as success. But success is as personal to you as your goals. If your purpose and ideal life involve you being a stay-at-home mum, and you do this, you're successful. We should, therefore, ignore societies definition of success and instead, take the time to focus on our definition of success.

I came across the following anecdote which shows how relative success can be:

At age 4, success is not peeing your pants
At age 12, success is having friends
At age 17, success is having a driving licence
At age 20, success is having sex
At age 35, success is having money
At age 50, success is having money
At age 60, success is having sex
At age 70, success is having a driving licence
At age 75, success is having friends
At age 85, success is not peeing your pants

Success means different things to different people. It might mean accumulating wealth, having a business that makes a certain amount of money or getting to the top level in their field. To others, it could be passing an exam, learning to play a new song on the piano or raising children. It could be overcoming your fears and taking action, doing your best and not giving up. Success can mean so many different things. But which definition can be most beneficial to us?

Success vs achievement

Most people confuse success and achievement and use their achievements to define their success. But there is a difference between success and achievement. Achievement is a one-time outcome, something you can strive for in the future, a tangible goal with a clearly defined measurable. If you think you can only be successful once you've achieved something, you say things like "I will be successful when I have £1 million in the bank". The problem with this type of definition is you are putting off your success to a future point, effectively saying "I will be successful when…". There is a better way to define success. Separate it from achievement. Achievement focuses on the future. We live in the present, so base your definition of success in the present.

Success, therefore, is a feeling or state of being where you say in the present tense "I am successful". If you are successful in the present moment, it is dependent on your actions today. Instead of saying "I will be successful when…", you say "I am successful because…". So, you'd change "I will be successful when I have a net worth of £1 million" to "I am successful because I save and invest 10% of my income each month and am on track to meet my financial targets". It is a much more rewarding and motivating way to view success. You can be successful today, even before you've achieved any goals. You are successful as long as you are working towards your goals.

Lesson summary:

1. Ignore societies definition of success and instead, take the time to focus on your definition.
2. Learn the difference between success and achievement to understand that you can be successful in the present moment.

Lesson #92: Celebrate your success

"The more you praise and celebrate your life, the more there is in life to celebrate" Oprah Winfrey

Punishing ourselves for bad behaviour usually comes very easy to us. No matter what the mistake is, we beat ourselves up over it. But when we accomplish something good, we can often struggle to celebrate it. However small an accomplishment, we should take the time to celebrate it and feel good about ourselves for doing it.

We must realise that our long-term goals aren't going to happen overnight and that the small wins are significant steps along the path. When you've completed a task, it's all too easy to place your focus on the next one and forget to stop and reflect on what you've just achieved. But if you ignore the win, you miss a vital opportunity to inspire yourself on to even greater successes. We crave a reward for our efforts. Without celebrating, we don't receive the reward. Any effort that goes unrewarded is unlikely to be repeated. We've just worked hard and received nothing for it. But when you celebrate and reward yourself, you have something to show for your efforts, and so the action is repeated in the expectation of receiving another reward.

Celebrating small wins along the way will motivate and inspire you to reach the next small success and the next. These small wins are what add up to make you achieve your big life-changing wins.

The success cycle relies on celebrating your victories. When any action from you results in a positive outcome, take the time to celebrate it. In doing so, you will make yourself feel good, which in turn will lead to more action and so the cycle continues. The cycle is illustrated below:

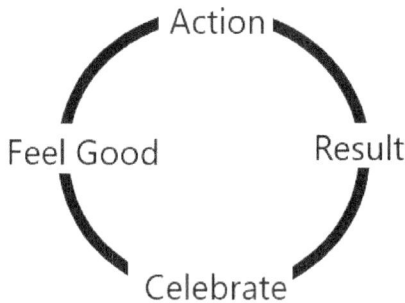

Action

Feel Good   Result

Celebrate

When you achieve something, however small it may be, go through the following steps to help you appreciate the significance of it:

1. Notice the win. You must acknowledge it as a win. At the end of each day, ask yourself what you achieved that day. You don't have to be flawless every day, just look for small measures of improvement. Remind yourself that you don't need to be a master by day 5 and this will ensure you are one by day 5000.

2. Think why you set this goal? It's easy to forget why a goal is important. Remind yourself of your why to bring significance to the task.

3. Relate the task to your vision and ask whether this success brings you closer to it.

4. List all the benefits of completing this action and achieving this result.

5. Realise that all your hard work was worth all the time and effort invested.

6. Reflect on how you feel about completing this task and observe the progress that you've made towards your goals.

Lesson summary:

1. Celebrate your small win to inspire further action.

Lesson #93: Forget the mistake, remember the lesson

"Experience is a hard teacher because she gives the test first, the lesson afterward" Vernon Law

It's said that the best way to learn is through making mistakes. Some people would argue that an even better way is to learn from the mistakes of others; however, I would disagree. When the error is yours, and it costs you in time, effort, or money, it hurts much more than hearing about someone else making the same mistake. So, when it's your mistake, it has a lasting impression on you. It's natural to beat yourself up about the mistake, especially when it's avoidable. But when you make mistakes, the most important thing to remember is the lesson.

Feedback lessons

You will make mistakes. It's important that you do. But don't dwell on them or punish yourself for them. Instead, think about the lesson the mistake is teaching you. This is valuable feedback that contributes to your overall success. The lesson could teach you more about yourself, your beliefs or values. It could be that now you've achieved a goal, you've realised it wasn't what you wanted. You may have found that writing your goals in a particular way was more helpful to you, so review all your other goals and write them the same way. If you achieved a goal too easily, make the next goal harder. Were your timelines realistic? What have you learnt that can be used to improve your other goals? Is there a particular skill you need to focus more time and attention on? As you start to achieve your goals, you'll find that your other goals will change to reflect the growth in your experience and knowledge. Some will no longer hold any attraction to you or your long-term vision, so let them go without feeling any guilt or shame. You are never a finished task.

Lesson summary:

1. You will make mistakes, but when you look back on them, remember the lesson rather than beating yourself up for the mistake.
2. Always feedback what you learn.

CONCLUSION

"It's all going to be fine in the end, if it's not yet fine, then it's not yet the end" Oscar Wilde

We've covered a lot in this book. If I had to summarise the main message in one sentence, it would be to think about and write down what you want, make plans to achieve it and work on it every day. In this conclusion are some final lessons that I consider important to living a fulfilled and successful life. I hope you can find the same value in them as I do, and they contribute towards a more fulfilled life for you.

Lesson #94: Time is your most precious resource

"The most precious thing a human being has to give is time. There is so very little of it, after all, in life" Edith Schaeffer

An important fact of life is that your time here is limited. Having a finite amount of time gives meaning to life. If it were unlimited, we wouldn't value it in the way we do. 2,680,560,000. That's the number of seconds in the average person's life. Your clock starts counting down from the moment you're born. This clock cannot be controlled, paused, or extended. The only thing you can control is how you chose to use it. Time is the most valuable resource you have, so spend it doing things that bring you joy and happiness as often as you can because one day, your clock will stop.

Imagine that you've won a competition where at midnight every day, £86,400 would be deposited in your bank account. But there's a catch. You would lose anything you didn't spend by midnight the next day. The bank can close your account at any time, without warning, and you won't get a new one. Would you spend the entire £86,400 each day? If so, how would you choose to spend it? Would you take care of your health and well-being? Or invest in your education? Perhaps you'd spend some on your family and donate some to help those who need it? These are all good causes, and I'm sure you'd be willing to spend some of your money on them. But would you give it away so easily to those who demand it from you? Or would you spend £15,000 each day to watch TV?

We all have a bank account just like this. Instead of receiving £86,400, we receive 86,400 seconds. But something strange happens when we replace the pound sign with seconds. Most of us would answer the questions above very differently. We don't spend much time looking after our health and well-being or improving ourselves. We don't volunteer to help those in need. What we do instead is give priority to the things in life that distract us from what's important. We work long hours. Family and health take a back seat. And when we're not working, we're spending most of our time sitting in front of a TV or phone screen.

Perhaps you don't value your time in the same way you value money? If this is you, then you need to get clear on the relative value of time vs. money. You can always make more money, but you only have a finite amount of time. Treat your time with the respect it deserves and use it intentionally on the things that matter most to you. Ask yourself, if I died right now, would I be OK with that? Most will answer no because there are too many unresolved problems, ambitions, and dreams not realised. There's too much about our lives that we haven't had the chance to explore or enjoy yet. Only two things are certain, we are alive right now, and at some point, we won't be. You cannot afford to waste a single second.

Lesson summary:

1. Time is your most precious resource so spend it doing the things that bring you joy and happiness as often as you can.

Lesson #95: Learn from the dying

"It is not death that a man should fear, but he should fear never beginning to live" Marcus Aurelius

Death is a subject none of us like to think or talk about. It's only when we lose someone that it brings home the reality that we will one day leave this world behind. I want to use this lesson to think and talk about death, instead of trying as hard as we can to pretend it doesn't exist, so we can learn valuable lessons, not in how to die, but in how to live.

1. Accept that death is inevitable

However unwelcome death may be, it will eventually come. Some people spend their whole life trying to resist this inevitability. There's nothing we can do to change the fact that we will one day die. The only thing we can do is accept it and use it to live the best we can. When you do this, you focus your thoughts and energy on the thing you can affect, how you live today. It gives you the perspective to see what's important in life. Things that previously seemed important are exposed as worthless in the context of death. So, instead of seeing death as a negative, our limited time here is what gives life meaning and value.

2. Life is now

The start and end of your life are like the cover of a book. Significant as they may feel, neither matters as much as the story that fills the pages in between. If you knew that today was your last day, how would you choose to live it? More importantly, why are you not living that way already? If you knew it was going to be your last meal, would you rush through it while you watched TV, or would you savour every mouthful? If it was going to be the last time you saw your friends and family, would you treat them any differently? Why does it have to be the last time for you to choose to relish the moment? Live every moment as if it were your last. Don't let anything pass by unappreciated. We rush through life and forget that the time to live is now.

3. Life is a rental

Life is a zero-sum game. This means we come in with nothing, and we leave with nothing. Why then do we hold on so tight to the things in life when sooner or later they will all be gone? Everything we are ever given must someday be taken away. We never truly own anything; we are simply custodians. Accept this, and you will find freedom in it. If nothing is yours, then nothing can be lost. So, let things come and go and experience them while they last. Love them, appreciate them but when it's time to move on, let them go. When you let everything flow in and out of your life, you may find you end up with more. When something moves out of your life, it creates space for new experiences to move in. Choose to rent every experience that comes your way, enjoy it fully but let nothing own you. All of life becomes ours to enjoy, but not to keep.

Lesson summary:

1. Death can teach us valuable lessons about how to live.
2. Accept death to help gain perspective on what's important in life, live in the moment and without unhealthy attachments to possessions.

Lesson #96: Don't take regrets to the grave

"Live is short, break the rules, forgive quickly, kiss slowly, love truly, laugh uncontrollably, and never regret anything that made you smile. Twenty years from now, you will be more disappointed by the things you didn't do than by the ones you did. So, throw off the bowlines. Sail away from the safe harbour. Catch the trade winds in your sails. Explore. Dream. Discover." Mark Twain

At the end of our lives, we will ask questions and think about our regrets to determine whether we had a good life. If you can figure out what these questions and regrets will be today, you can make sure you'll be happy with the answers at the end. Bronnie Ware, a palliative care nurse who cared for the terminally ill, wrote a book based on the regrets of the dying. She concluded that the top 5 regrets were:

1. I wish I'd had the courage to live a life true to myself, not the life others expected of me
2. I wish I hadn't worked so hard
3. I wish I'd had the courage to express my feelings
4. I wish I'd stayed in touch with my friends
5. I wish that I had let myself be happier

However old you are, do a regret test once a year. Imagine you have a time machine and you can go forward into the future to the day of your death. You walk through the hospital corridors and onto the ward where you're staying. As you walk through the door, you see your older self lying on the bed, wrinkled and grey, surrounded by your family. You walk up next to the bed and look down at yourself lying there, about to leave this world behind. You ask your older self what regrets they have. What would they say? Think about that for a moment. You have minutes left to live and no time left to resolve these regrets. Let that sink in. You will pass away, knowing you could have been more and done more with your life. But it's too late as you slip away.

Now bring yourself back to the present. If you have a good imagination and were able to visualise yourself on your deathbed, you'll be so grateful when you bring your mind back to the present moment and realise that you now have the chance to do something with the time you have left. You have the opportunity to change the future. Don't become that version of yourself you just imagined. Think about the regrets you might have, write them down and regularly refer to them as motivation for becoming the person you want to be and achieving your goals and dreams. Embrace your mortality and use it to act now for a better life. Don't take regrets to the grave.

Lesson summary:

1. Think about the regrets you might have at the end of your life by doing a regret test once a year.
2. Do something about those regrets today, while you still have the time.

Lesson #97: Self-development matters

"You can't go back and change the beginning, but you can start where you are and change the ending" C.S Lewis

During my research for this book, I came across something called Maslow's Hierarchy of Needs. It describes our needs, starting at the bottom of the pyramid with our basic physiological and safety requirements such as oxygen, water, food, sleep, and security. These are what we need to survive. Next, are psychological needs, including belonging and love needs then esteem needs, such as a sense of accomplishment. Finally, at the top of the pyramid is self-actualisation or self-fulfilment needs. This is the highest level on your hierarchy of needs. When you fulfil all levels of the hierarchy, you feel that all your needs in life are fulfilled, and you are achieving your full potential.

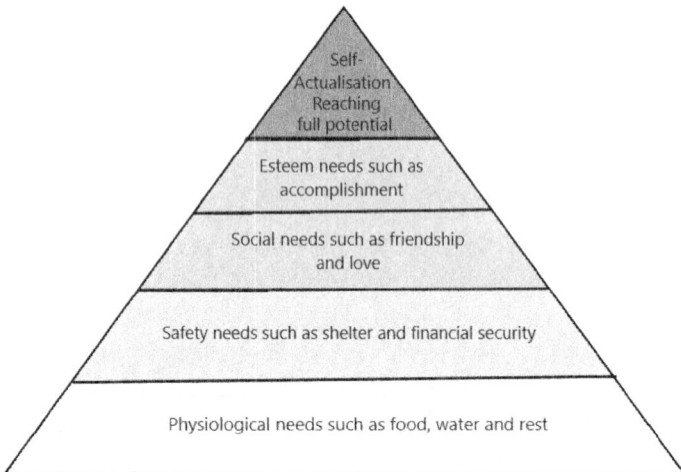

The hierarchy can be divided into two main sets of needs: deficiency and growth. The first four levels are deficiency needs, and the top-level is a growth need. Deficiency needs arise due to deprivation and motivate people when they are unmet. Our bodies are wired to tell us when something is missing. For example, go without water and thirst will motivate you to find it. When a deficit need has been satisfied, it will go away, and our actions become directed at the next level. A growth need does not stem from a lack of something but rather from a desire to grow as a person. Every person is capable and has the desire to move up the hierarchy. It should be your aim to reach the top level of the hierarchy to experience complete fulfilment. We are all capable of it; however, Maslow estimated that only two per cent of people reach the state. Reach the top level, and you achieve the final thing you need to experience a fulfilled life.

Personal growth matters; it completes you. Don't stand still. Don't watch the next 5 or 10 years of your life go by and be the same person in the same place. Make growth and development an essential part of your life. Think about your ideal vision, set goals, and intentionally work towards them every day. You don't need to take massive action, small and persistent steps in the right direction will compound over the years, and it may only be when you look back that you realise how far you've come. You can change your life for the better. The best part of your story is that the next page is blank, and you get to write it. You can start a new chapter at any moment. Start now.

Lesson summary:

1. The hierarchy of needs describes our requirements for a fulfilled life, and when all levels are met, we experience the best from life.
2. Personal growth and development are key to ensuring your self-fulfilment needs at the top of the hierarchy are met.

Lesson #98: Don't get cooked in the squat

"I didn't come this far to only come this far" Tom Brady

It's now over to you. You can have everything you've dreamt of. Except they no longer have to be just dreams. They can be well thought out and meaningful goals with plans for how to achieve them.

In his book *Goals*, Zig Ziglar tells a story from his childhood. When over at a friend's house for dinner, the cook bought out some biscuits, but they hadn't risen. He looked at them and said, "Maude, what on earth happened to the biscuits?" She replied "Well, I'll tell you about those biscuits. They squatted to rise, but they just got cooked in the squat". There's a very real danger that you will get cooked in the squat. I'm talking about one final hurdle that you must overcome, and it's a big one. If you're like most people, you'll read the lessons and get inspired to act. But the last hurdle is the gap between wanting to change and working to make that change happen. You've prepared yourself well by reading to the end of this book, but unless you take that first step, you'll be cooked in the squat. You've got to take action. The stuff in this book is worthless unless you put it into action. This lesson is designed to help you do that, so this book doesn't just inspire you to think about a better life, it inspires you to act for a better life.

Focus on the next 90 days

Think of the next 90 days as a testing period, where you'll start seeing results that will convince you this stuff works. Prove to yourself you are good enough to do it and in control of your future. Imagine it's 90 days from now and it's been the best 90 days of your life. What does it look like? What has changed? What results did you get? What goals have you made a start on? What goals have you achieved? If you just spent the next 90 days working through the exercises in this book, how much more clarity do you think your life would have? Now write down the action steps to make those things happen. Then write down the first small step and do it within the next 24 hours. The 90-day challenge gets you to take immediate action. The first 90 days will be the hardest. If you can take action over the next 90 days, you'll have everything you need to continue that over the rest of your life. The next 90 days are the entrance fee you have to pay.

It's time to stop thinking about a better life and start living it. Now is your time. If you say it isn't a good time, then what you are saying is there will never be a good time. Don't stress about the things you can't change. Focus on what is within your control. Your past is research and development for the great life that lies ahead of you. You have the roadmap that can take you where you desire. It takes time and effort but the sooner you start, the sooner you'll arrive where you want to be. Act now, and as you begin to see small changes, it will motivate you to continue. Lay the path to your vision brick by brick, and when you look back in 10 years, you'll see the amazing journey you've been on and the beautiful thing your life has become. The content of this book is inspired by many of the world's most successful people. It has helped them move to the next level in life. It has helped me move to the next level in life. And now you have it in your hands. Where will it take you?

Lesson summary:

1.   The final hurdle is deciding to act.
2.   Focus on the next 90 days to inspire immediate action.

Lesson #99: Elevate your ending

"Anyone can deliver a happy ending, just give the characters everything they want" Robert McKee

I'd like you to think about all the things you've achieved and imagine how you would feel achieving all your future goals. You've reached the end and have everything you wanted. But did you actually get what you wanted or perhaps something more?

Consider the endings to some of the best films you've seen. Screenwriters understand the importance of endings, and they know that the best endings are not always happy in the traditional sense. Happy endings are easy. You just give the characters what they've been chasing the whole film. But to deliver a truly inspiring end, you should provide the emotion you've been promised but with a rush of unexpected insight. That often comes when the main character finally understands an emotionally complex truth. John August who wrote the screenplay for Charlie and the Chocolate Factory argues that this more sophisticated form of elevation is the secret to the success of Pixar films such as Up, Cars and the Toy Story films: *"Every Pixar movie has its protagonist achieving the goal he wants, only to realise it is not what they need. Typically, this leads them to let go of what they thought they wanted – the house, the piston cup, Andy – to get what they need – a true yet unlikely companion, real friends, a lifetime together with friends"*. Such emotional complexity turns out to be central to the most elevated endings. It makes your ending meaningful.

The best ends don't just leave us happy. Instead, they produce something richer, leaving us with a better understanding of what is important in life. The possibility that by discarding what we thought we wanted, we've got what we need. I hope that by going through the steps in this book, you have identified what you want and how to get it, but most importantly, I hope it gives you what you need from life.

My goal in writing this book was to share the knowledge that has pulled me out of the lowest point in my life. If you've taken one thing from the book that will help improve your life in any way, then I have succeeded. If this book has inspired you to take control of your future, please pass it on to someone that you would like to inspire. I have developed a set of supplementary documents to help guide you through the various exercises in this book. If you would like copies of these, please email me at memoriesnotdreams100@gmail.com.

First lines in books are very carefully thought out as they attempt to hook the reader. Final lines are just as important as they should elevate and inspire the reader into action. It

should encapsulate the essence of the entire book and answer the question the reader had when they picked up the book. So, in an attempt to capture all of the above, here is my final line and it makes up the last lesson of the book. Thanks for reading.

Lesson #100: Die with memories, not dreams

Printed in Great Britain
by Amazon